THE OFFICIAL COMPANION TO THE 1999 CRICKET WORLD CUP

ROB STEEN

BOXTREE

WISDEN

Chapter 1

For Openers

'It was just short of nine o'clock and the streetlights were going on all round Old Trafford…This before a crowd of 23,520 and with 459 runs scored in a single day. I understand that there is a similar game played at Lord's where only 100 runs may be scored in a day before a mere sprinkling of onlookers and the players insist on coming off the field when a cloud passes over the sun in broad daylight. Is there any known connection between the two?'

Perversity, thy name is cricket. Peter Ecker, a resident of Breaston near Derby, was moved to pen those sly, only slightly exaggerated sentiments to the *Guardian* in 1971, in the wake of the Gillette Cup semi-final between Lancashire and Gloucestershire, the first manifestation of the oft-derided 'instant' game to stir rather than prick the public imagination. Hell, the BBC even delayed the *Nine O'Clock News* to capture the climax. Four summers later, nigh-on a century after the inaugural Test match, that imagination found a new, more commodious receptacle – The World Cup of Cricket. And so the conversion began in earnest: from toffs' game to people's game.

It is tempting to wonder, nevertheless, whether the fates wanted their say in this bright new tomorrow. Had the rains that lashed the inflation-riddled England of May 1975 persisted – in each of their opening four championship fixtures Yorkshire lost an entire day's play (less half an hour) – who can say how the pilot would have fared? Even then, a soggy final could have undone everything. There was also a rival attraction in town: the Beach Boys at Wembley or West Indies v Australia? I admit it: I was torn. The idea of getting drenched beneath the Twin Towers held vastly fewer fears than suffering a similar fate at Lord's. And who knew if the Wilson boys would ever make it back to this particular beach?

Not until nine o'clock that morning did I make up my mind (my stepfather had a substitute lined up to join him in the Mound Stand, so there was only a moderate portion of guilt involved). God only knows (hah) why I plumped for Lillee and Lloyd over California's concept of good vibrations (boom and, furthermore, boom). It was probably the prospect of seeing the Aussies get a damn good stuffing. But, thankfully, I did, even if I did walk those 400-odd yards back home before Lillian Thomson gave the tale that unforgettable late twist. The sun did the decent thing, donning his hat and keeping it on as a momentous occasion was blessed with a contest to match. One of the many enraptured onlookers was Kerry Francis Bullmore Packer, the milkshake-loving, chukka-scoring media tycoon without whom so much of what followed might never have happened. For it was on that historic day that the seeds were sown for World Series Cricket, breeding ground for white balls, puce pyjamas and twilight thrashes, not to mention copious amounts of fear and loathing. Year Zero was upon us.

Unlike any other sport you may care to mention, the sheer length and breadth of cricket's loftiest form of expression renders a World Test Cup more or less impracticable. Only in 1912 had toes been dipped: the Triangular Tournament in England, wherein the hosts, Australia and South Africa, the only members of the Imperial Cricket Conference (as was), met each other three times on a league basis. Rain ravaged three of the contests and the experiment was never repeated. Sixty years on, it was abundantly clear that the only way such an event could be staged – indeed, the only way cricket could continue to hold the attention of subsequent generations – would be for the game itself to change, to adapt to a society increasingly spoilt for choice and starved of concentration. Or at least diversify. And so it came to pass that, prodded by the replenishing effect the Gillette Cup and the John Player Sunday League were having on county gates and coffers, the World Cup was hatched.

No other sport has regenerated itself by dint of such complete and utter reinvention. Yet even now, as we look forward to the seventh running of cricket's very own Grand National, the biggest and bravest yet (if not quite the brashest), the curmudgeons are still up in arms, still scoffing, still deriding. Mickey Mouse cricket, they sneer. An activity for athletic simpletons. A rock 'n' roll abomination tolerated solely because, as the golden goose, it supports the sonatas and fugues. Luckily, those who really matter, the spectators, have more catholic tastes.

The past 23 years have seen cricket evolve into the most adaptable and equable of all sports. Innovation, moreover, has been almost exclusively the province of the so-called bastard offspring. Much as it removes some of the languid, time-stopping beauty, condensing cricket magnifies its complexities, puts fiercer pressure on its combatants. Every ball counts. Ask a captain which is the more demanding, plotting a campaign in a one-day game or a first-class version and he will probably shoot you the sort of pitying look he normally reserves for his daughter's ailing hamster. During the early World Cups, teams for the most part were dead ringers for their five-day counterparts. Then came the emergence of the bits 'n' pieces all-rounder, proficient enough in neither major discipline to command a regular Test place yet remarkably handy over the short haul. Then came the 'pinch-hitter', a batsman prepared to sacrifice his wicket if it meant giving his side a rollicking send-off: a breath of freshest air. Even though the deadline for this book precluded knowledge of the nominated squads (apologies in advance for any inadvertent misinformation), it is a fair bet that the distinction between the two branches of our favourite poplar will be ever more vividly reflected during the course of the 1999 Cricket World Cup. Of the England XI that lost the Emirates Triangular Tournament final at Lord's last August, only four constituents were Test regulars.

The one great advantage cricket World Cups have over their equivalent in football's muddied oafery – aside, naturally, from cricket's infinite superiority as a competitive art – is their comparatively diminutive fields. Thirty-two nations participated in France 98, culled from hundreds; even when there were half that many, the qualification process would take well over a year. As a consequence, many a leading light has been unable to appear, let alone shine – George Best to name but the most regrettable instance. Others, like that Portuguese man o' war, Eusebio, make but fleeting visitations. The intimacy of the cricket circuit, for all that its participants are almost as far-flung, means that the best strut their stuff almost without exception. Games, moreover, are proportionally more meaningful; expanding the field from one minnow to three has done little to change that. Quality 1, Quantity 0.

Structural tinkerings have been a regular feature of past World Cups, and the latest brings one particularly welcome progression, namely the Super Six. Previously, the latter stages had been conventional knockouts, penalizing those (eg. South Africa in 1996) who have one fallow hour amid days of plenty; in addition to pitting the best against each other more often, an intermediate group stage should also sort out wheat from chaff with a more thorough sense of justice. Whoever ultimately triumphs, the examination promises to be more equitable as well as more searching. If, in the fullness of time, the Super Six does go the way of the second phase implemented for the 1974, 1978 and 1982 FIFA tourneys, it won't be for the same reason. In limited-overs cricket, playing for a draw is not an option.

World Cups purport to be celebrations – of the best, of the worthiest, of the game itself. Which is why the presence of Bangladesh, Kenya and Scotland, whatever the score-cards might infer to the contrary, is so critical. The 1999 Cricket World Cup is as much about spreading gospels as bets. And the more disciples, surely, the better. An enthusiasm shared, after all, is an enthusiasm squared. Right now, Kenya are where their continent's footballers were, say, 15 years ago; who can say they won't be the Nigeria of the 2007 World Cup? Which is why, speaking parochially, the last World Cup of the millennium is so crucial to cricket's future in England. It is an opportunity to spread that gospel, one that probably won't arise again until Alec Stewart is serving his country as chairman of selectors, coach and chef.

For the benefit of Mr Pom there will be a show tonight. And tomorrow night. And the next. And the next. The Waughs and Flowers will all be there. A splendid time is guaranteed for all.

Rob Steen
London
January 1999

Chapter 2

Match Schedule

Not for the first time – nor, one strongly suspects, the last – the World Cup has been restructured, happily much for the better. The introduction of the Super Six stage, whereby each of the three leading teams in Group A plays a further three games against their counterparts in Group B to decide the semi-finalists, has increased the number of matches while reducing the knockout element. Theoretically at least, this will benefit the better teams and public alike. The advent of a quarter-final round in 1996, while adding to the drama, was not considered an unmitigated success, albeit mostly because Pakistan were eliminated at that juncture by fellow co-hosts India, who compounded the sin by entering the match with an inferior record.

At the time of going to press, the majority of the 42 matches were already sold out. Fortunately, television and radio coverage is of the wall-to-wall variety.

Notes:

1. All games allotted two days, except the final which has three.
2. If either semi-final is severely disrupted by the weather, the sides with the best record in the Super Six stage will go through.

World Cup Schedule

Group A *(First three teams qualify)*

Date	Match	Venue	Previous World Cup Result
14 May	**England v Sri Lanka**	Lord's	5–1
15 May	**India v South Africa**	Hove	0–1
	Zimbabwe v Kenya	Taunton	N/A
18 May	**England v Kenya**	Canterbury	N/A
19 May	**Sri Lanka v South Africa**	Northampton	1–0
	India v Zimbabwe	Leicester	6–0
22 May	**England v South Africa**	The Oval	2–1
	Zimbabwe v Sri Lanka	Worcester	0–2
23 May	**Kenya v India**	Bristol	N/A
25 May	**England v Zimbabwe**	Trent Bridge	0–1
26 May	**Sri Lanka v India**	Taunton	2–0 (1 No Result)
	South Africa v Kenya	Amsterdam	N/A
29 May	**England v India**	Edgbaston	3–1
	Zimbabwe v South Africa	Chelmsford	0–1
30 May	**Sri Lanka v Kenya**	Southampton	1–0

Group B *(First three teams qualify)*

Date	Match	Venue	Previous World Cup Result
16 May	**Australia v Scotland**	Worcester	N/A
	West Indies v Pakistan	Bristol	5–1
17 May	**New Zealand v Bangladesh**	Chelmsford	N/A
20 May	**Australia v New Zealand**	Cardiff	3–1
	Pakistan v Scotland	Chester-le-Street	N/A
21 May	**West Indies v Bangladesh**	Dublin	N/A
23 May	**Australia v Pakistan**	Headingley	2–2
24 May	**West Indies v New Zealand**	Southampton	2–1
	Scotland v Bangladesh	Edinburgh	N/A
27 May	**West Indies v Scotland**	Leicester	N/A
	Australia v Bangladesh	Chester-le-Street	N/A
28 May	**New Zealand v Pakistan**	Derby	1–4
30 May	**West Indies v Australia**	Old Trafford	5–2
31 May	**Scotland v New Zealand**	Edinburgh	N/A
	Pakistan v Bangladesh	Northampton	N/A

Second Stage *Super Six (Four sides with most points progress)*

4 June	**Group A (2nd) v Group B (2nd)**	The Oval
5 June	**Group A (1st) v Group B (1st)**	Trent Bridge
6 June	**Group A (3rd) v Group B (3rd)**	Headingley
8 June	**Group A (2nd) v Group B (1st)**	Old Trafford
9 June	**Group A (3rd) v Group B (2nd)**	Lord's
10 June	**Group A (1st) v Group B (3rd)**	Edgbaston
11 June	**Group A (3rd) v Group B (1st)**	The Oval
12 June	**Group A (2nd) v Group B (3rd)**	Trent Bridge
13 June	**Group A (1st) v Group B (2nd)**	Headingley

Semi-finals

16 June   Old Trafford
Semi-final 1: 1st Super Six v 4th (tbc)

17 June   Edgbaston
Semi-final 2: 2nd Super Six v 3rd (tbc)

Final

20 June   Lord's

Previous Meetings at a Glance

	1975	1979	1983	1987	1992	1996	Total
England v Sri Lanka			2-0	2-0	1-0	0-1	5-1
England v South Africa					2-0	0-1	2-1
England v Zimbabwe					0-1		0-1
England v India	1-0		0-1	1-0	1-0		3-1
India v South Africa					0-1		0-1
Zimbabwe v Kenya						1-0	1-0
West Indies v Pakistan	1-0	1-0	1-0	1-1	1-0		5-1
Sri Lanka v South Africa					1-0		1-0
India v Zimbabwe			2-0	2-0	1-0	1-0	6-0
Australia v New Zealand				2-0	0-1	1-0	3-1
Zimbabwe v Sri Lanka					0-1	0-1	0-2
Kenya v India						0-1	0-1
Australia v Pakistan	1-0	0-1		1-0	0-1		2-2
West Indies v New Zealand	1-0	1-0			0-1		2-1
Sri Lanka v India		1-0			NR	1-0	2-0 (1 NR)
New Zealand v Pakistan			1-1		0-2	0-1	1-4
Zimbabwe v South Africa					0-1		0-1
Sri Lanka v Kenya						1-0	1-0
West Indies v Australia	2-0		2-0		0-1	1-1	5-2

Other Notable Match-ups

	1975	1979	1983	1987	1992	1996	Total
England v Australia	0-1	1-0		0-1	1-0		2-2
England v West Indies		0-1		2-0	1-0		3-1
India v Pakistan					1-0	1-0	2-0

Chapter 3

A–Z

Aims

To score more runs in your allotted 50 overs than the opposition. Not that this is always sufficient to guarantee the spoils (see **Calculations**).

Bedi, Bishen

The Prince of a Thousand Patkas, owner of a bowling action so silky it made Fred Astaire look like a clodhopper. One-day cricket was going to be the death of the spinner, they said. Batsmen would regard them as fodder, they said. Flight and turn would be sacrificed on the altar of the dot ball, they said. Pish. Granted, Allan Border's really-rather-brisk slow left-armers and Eddie Hemmings' pancake-flat off-breaks decided the 1987 final and semi-finals with scarcely a nod to the purists. All the same, the best have prospered, notably Mushtaq Ahmed, the Pakistani googly maestro who turned the 1992 final, and Shane Warne, Ol' Golden Wrist himself, whose spell

against West Indies won that tumultuous, utterly unforgettable 1996 semi-final for Australia. Bedi, the Punjabi whose elegant artistry failed to disguise a fiery if sizable belly, showed them all the way.

Doubtless bridling after being omitted from the Indian XI for the World Cup's inaugural fixture on 11 June 1975, against England at Lord's, the languid left-armer faced the admittedly less-than-mighty East Africans at Headingley. 'I am not unhappy to be hit for six sixes,' he once insisted. 'I want batsmen to play shots. Only then can I get them out.' On this occasion he settled for something more relevant. Of his apportioned dozen overs, eight were maidens; all told he conceded just six runs, and without the vaguest hint of compromise. Bishen Singh Bedi firing the ball in at leg-stump? Right, and Jean-Claude Van Damme wears a woolly vest.

Even with the reduction of the number of

Full World Cup League Table

	P	W	L	No Result	% (wins/completed matches)
West Indies	37	25	12	0	67.57
South Africa	15	10	5	0	66.67
England	40	25	14	1	64.10
Australia	37	22	15	0	59.46
Pakistan	37	21	15	1	58.33
New Zealand	35	19	16	0	54.29
India	36	18	17	1	51.43
Sri Lanka	31	10	20	1	33.33
Kenya	6	1	4	1	20.00
UAE	5	1	4	0	20.00
Zimbabwe	26	3	22	1	12.00
Canada	3	0	3	0	–
East Africa	3	0	3	0	–
Holland	5	0	5	0	–
Bangladesh	–	–	–	–	–
Scotland	–	–	–	–	–

All records based on all official matches, as defined by the ICC.

The match between Zimbabwe and Kenya at Patna in 1996 counts together with the match that was abandoned on the previous day between the two sides.
★ = not out batsman or unbeaten partnership.

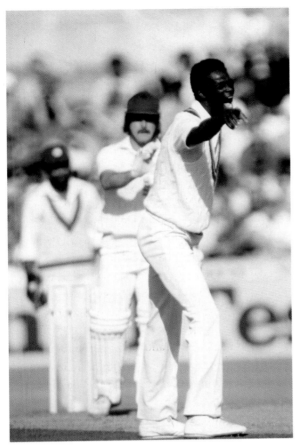

The saint of St Vincent: Winston Davis

overs available to each bowler – 10 since matches slimmed down from 60 overs to 50 in 1987 – nobody has ever proved quite so suffocatingly mean. In the next game, against New Zealand, he offered a near-repeat, sending down a further half-dozen maidens. Had he managed more than one wicket, mind, India might well have reached the semis. As it was, Glenn Turner was content to see him off and plunder his lesser brethren, the sly old bird for once outwitted.

Calculations

The most annoying fly in the World Cup ointment has undoubtedly been the methods used to decide matches in the event of proceedings being disrupted – by rain, for example. Based on average totals made for specific numbers of overs, and taking into account one-day internationals played worldwide over a decade or more, the process of adjusting targets is known as the Duckworth-Lewis system, after its English inventors, and has since been adopted as the universal norm. The one drawback is that it is possible for the chasing side to pass their opponents but still lose.

Davis, Winston

The owner of the best bowling return in World Cup history was an unlikely candidate indeed. As the sixth and least experienced member of the West Indian pace battery, comparatively little was expected of this wiry, whippy St Vincentian when he was summoned to the front against Australia at Headingley in 1983, as one of two replacements for the injured Joel Garner and Malcolm Marshall. Some shoes.

Australia, 114 for two chasing 253, had recovered well on a substandard pitch after seeing Graeme Wood sustain concussion when struck by a short one from Michael Holding. So much so, they had just walloped 59 off the previous eight overs as David Hookes cut loose, ably supported by Graeme Yallop; were the holders about to suffer their maiden defeat in the competition? Davis had already given up 37 runs when he picked up his second wicket; he wound up taking six of the last seven for 14, dismissing Australia for 151 and finishing with the somewhat quixotic analysis of 10.3-0-51-7.

At Old Trafford the following summer he caused havoc of a decidedly less pleasurable hue, administering the blow that fractured Paul Terry's forearm and ended the Hampshire batsman's fledgling Test career. The fates proved nothing if not vengeful. Last year, while clearing the ground to build a church in his home village in St Vincent, a branch fell on him. He is now a tetraplegic, denied the use of arms or legs. References to his plight by Matthew Engel – Davis spent several summers at the writer's beloved Northants, albeit not long enough to earn him a benefit – stirred readers of the *Guardian* and *Wisden Cricket Monthly* to make generous donations, enough to purchase a wheelchair and transport back to England, to join his family in Worcester. Seldom has the greasy pole been greasier.

Economy Rate

Forget wickets (all right, just relegate them from the forefront of your mind). The only statistic that matters to a bowler in the one-day fray, or so they say, is the average number of runs he concedes per over – his economy rate. Hence the pre-eminence at past World Cups of the likes of Mohinder Amarnath, Gavin Larsen and Chris Harris, dibbly-dobbly merchants rarely entrusted with the ball in Tests or even at first-class level, where containment is of limited relevance, yet world-beaters when required merely to record dot balls. Confine the opposition to three an over and you're doing a bang-up job. True, there's no more effective deterrent than splattering a batsman's stumps. Better, though, to concede a total of 200 for one than dismiss the opposition for 201. Then again, ever since 1983, when Imran Khan insisted Pakistan find a place for leg-spinner Abdul Qadir, attack has generally been deemed the best means of defence. On the other hand, the most valuable bowlers in three out of the last four World Cup finals have been batsmen. A tricky one.

Fifteen

The number of overs at the start of an innings during which batsmen are granted licence to run amok with scarcely a finger lifted in defiance. During that period there can be no more than two fielders placed outside the fielding circle (a loose term), thus encouraging shots over the infield and into the untenanted acres beyond. First implemented in the 1992 tournament, the main legacy was the so-called pinch-hitter, whose antics so lit up the last World Cup. While this is a misnomer – in baseball, from whence the term is derived, the pinch-hitter is a substitute, not a member of the starting line-up – the philosophy is essentially the same. In cricket terms the title denotes a batsman of boisterous instincts elevated above a more sedate if technically superior colleague, the aim to take full advantage of the fielding restrictions. All the same, the most successful exploiter to date has been a bona fide opener, the Sri Lankan Sanath Jayasuriya. One of the by-products has been to de-emphasize the

importance of the last 10 overs, hitherto an undignified scramble. It is not uncommon to see 100 or more posted in those initial overs. Nor is it rare for the outcome of the match to be decided there and then.

Gower, David

Poached from BBC Television, for whom this tournament represents the last meaningful involvement with cricket for the foreseeable future after 60 years of commitment and quality, the most aesthetically pleasing of all English batsmen is now fronting the show for co-broadcasters Sky. He is a measured and whimsical critic, with a laid-back style of delivery that his onfield demeanor had portended, and his arrival compensates for Mark Nicholas's big-money transfer to Channel 4. The big difference between the two, of course, is that Nicholas never played for England, while Gower did so on 231 occasions. Not that this is any indicator of suitability. Nicholas makes up for what he lacks in first-hand experience with affection and enthusiasm. Gower is more detached, and hence less prone to putting his foot in it. Either way, Richie Benaud will be able to retire secure in the knowledge that he has at least two worthy heirs.

Hair, Darrell

For all the compelling claims of Javed Akhtar, whose trigger finger proved a mite too itchy for most tastes in England last summer, Australia's leading umpire can fairly claim to be the game's most controversial and fearless decision-maker. A long-standing member of the independent International Cricket Council panel that will preside over this tournament, he made headlines in the winter of 1995-96 when he no-balled Sri Lanka's Muttiah Muralitharan for throwing – and from the highly untraditional vantage point of the bowler's end. Three years later, in his autobiography, in an outburst he would publicly regret, he cited Muralitharan's action as 'diabolical' and said he would have no compunction whatsoever in calling him again, even though the freakish off-spinner had subsequently been given a clean bill of health. As a result he became the first umpire to be charged with bringing the game into disrepute. Elmo Rodrigopulle, the sports editor of the *Colombo Daily News*, never one to knowingly pull a punch, memorably described Hair as 'hair-braised' [sic] and 'an insult to Australia'. He also

proposed 'a sound kick up the behind' and that Hair 'should be sent scurrying like a hare'. After Hair had given him out at Lord's last summer, Mark Ramprakash was fined for accusing him of 'messing with people's careers'.

The fact remains that Hair's conduct is a fairly natural response to an era that has seen umpires, if not stripped of authority, then certainly reduced to their boxer shorts. Television has taken care of that – and thank goodness. If technology can reduce the number of palpably flawed decisions, which it is doing bit by grudging bit, so much the fairer, surely. Notions of the umpire as the ultimate arbiter are all very well, but it is the game that must be pandered to, not egos.

It is hard indeed to credit that television replays have been used in evidence only since 1992. Pandora's Box, however, was only allowed to creak open. First line decisions became the province of a third umpire armed with screen and walkie-talkie. Then, in 1997, catches were brought under his jurisdiction, though some onfield colleagues still declined to consult him, as they are empowered but ill-advised to do. There are even plans to relieve umpires of the responsibility for adjudging no-balls – much as the electronic beeper aids their counterparts in tennis – which would be a cause for unbridled joy. All of which should certainly give the lads a good deal more time to concentrate on getting those wides and lbws right. Leeway and understanding recommended.

ICC Trophy

Qualifying tournament under the auspices of the International Cricket Council (ICC) via which Bangladesh (winners), Kenya (runners-up) and Scotland (third) gained their World Cup berths for 1999. Devised as an aid to nurturing the game among the ICC's myriad associate members, its participants have ranged from the USA to the UAE, from Greenland to Gibraltar. National loyalties, mind, have been nothing if not flexible. In 1979, Fiji fielded Roderick Jepsen, a young chap of Danish parentage with first-class experience in New Zealand. When the Emirates took the trophy, ensuring a place at the last World Cup, they did so

World Cup Records

Highest total: 398-5, Sri Lanka v Kenya, Kandy 1996
Highest total batting second to win: 313-7, Sri Lanka v Zimbabwe, New Plymouth 1992
Highest match aggregate: 652 runs, Sri Lanka v Kenya, Kandy 1996
Largest margin of victory (runs): 202, England bt India, Lord's 1975
Largest margin of victory (wickets): 10, India v East Africa, Leeds 1975
West Indies v Zimbabwe, Birmingham 1983
West Indies v Pakistan, Melbourne 1992
Narrowest margin of victory (runs): 1, Australia bt India, Brisbane 1992
Australia bt India, Madras 1987
Narrowest margin of victory (wickets): 1, West Indies bt Pakistan, Birmingham 1975;
Pakistan bt West Indies, Melbourne 1992
Lowest total: 45, Canada v England, Manchester 1979
Slowest scoring rate (runs per over): 1.12, Canada 45 off 40.3 v England, Manchester 1979
Shortest completed innings: 30.3 overs, Australia v West Indies, Leeds 1983
Shortest match: 51 overs, Pakistan v UAE, Gujranwala 1996

amid all manner of chuntering about a side numbering just one true blue Arab. One of the more colourful characters was that multi-talented denizen of Papua New Guinea, Nigel Agonia, Seventh Day Adventist, government minister and, not unnaturally, team captain. 'Had it been not Nigel but Pat,' quipped Scyld Berry in *Wisden Cricket Monthly*, 'he could have qualified for Argentina.'

Jaffer, Salim

Beneficiary of the most sporting gesture in limited-overs history. Pakistan v West Indies, Lahore 1987, final over. The hosts require 14 to win a vital World Cup group match with their last pair together, the odds firmly on Viv Richards and his pals, whereupon Abdul Qadir unbuckles his swash: 12 off the first five balls and a remarkable victory in sight. As Courtney Walsh lopes into his delivery stride for the last time, he notices that the non-striker, Jaffer, is backing up a shade too enthusiastically. He knows full well he is perfectly entitled, by the letter if not the spirit of the law, to whip off the bails and run the miscreant out. Nor does he need any reminding that this would secure the spoils for his team as well as avert personal humiliation. To his undying credit he resists, contenting himself with a gentlemanly warning. In he lopes once more, Qadir heaves again and away skips the ball for the winning runs. West Indies are eliminated; a highly embarrassed Walsh finds himself showered with rupees, medals and a hand-woven carpet, not to say universal gratitude. An example to all – and still going strong.

Kingfisher

Brewing arm of the multinational United Breweries Group that sponsored West Indies during the 1996 World Cup and brought fresh meaning to the word gall. At first glance, for a team starved of domestic commercial support, such support was a godsend. Less welcome was the company's insistence on the players wearing corporate logos billing them as Kingfisher West Indies. They should have known better. Public reaction in the Caribbean was predictably irate; nor were Richie Richardson and his confrères overly amused. Kingfisher had to lump it; the relationship, needless to add, was brief. Tradition may do no more than create the illusion of permanence, but some illusions are worth preserving.

Laughter

Response of colleagues to Tariq Iqbal, Kenya's corpulent and incompetent wicket-keeper, whenever he dropped the ball against West Indies at Pune in 1996. Which was not infrequently... then he caught Brian Lara, setting up the most improbable World Cup result to date (see **Upsets**).

McKechnie, Brian

Victim of the most underhand ploy in limited-overs history. In the World Series Cup final at Melbourne in 1981, the thickset New Zealand all-rounder, famed more for his exploits as an All Black full-back, is confronted by a ticklish assignment: last ball, six to tie. Remote as the prospect is, Greg Chappell, the Australian captain, is in no mood to take a chance on being obliged to cram another game into an already overcrowded season. So he instructs his kid brother, Trevor, to deliver the ball underarm. 'No, mate,' urges wicket-keeper Rod Marsh, clearly aghast. 'Don't do it.' Greg is unwavering. 'I expected a lot of people would say, "tch, tch, not cricket"', he would reflect, 'but quite honestly I couldn't give a rat's tail.' Trevor takes four paces forward and propels the ball as if seeking a strike in a tenpin alley. McKechnie might as well swap his bat for a snooker cue. Ball blocked, he throws it in the air in exasperation. Bruce Edgar, the non-striker, brandishes a V-sign in Trevor's direction. Australia win but the name of Chappell is mud twice over. The New Zealand Prime Minister conveys his disgust. The lawmakers, mercifully, act swiftly to prevent a repeat.

No-ball

Sentence obliged to be passed on any delivery climbing higher than the striker's shoulder, regardless of whether he makes productive contact. Bouncers have no place in World Cups. Theoretically.

Oo-er

Common reaction among non-Australians to the principal hosts' official World Cup song of 1992. Released on the Sloggett label (double aargh), 'Who'll Rule the World?' comprised the sort of lyrics most songwriters get out of their system by the time they dispense with nappy and potty. To wit:

> *You're on the edge of your seat, feelings running high*
> *They're the best in the world, they make that white ball fly...*
> *Who'll rule the world, who'll rule the world?*
> *Gotta see who'll rule the world...*

Entirely scurrilous rumour has it that Sir Paul McCartney turned down the chance to pen a ditty for this year's tournament. Pity, really. He could have called it 'Can't Buy Me Hove'. Or 'Drive My Cardiff'.

Pyjama Parties

Disparaging *nom de plume* for limited-overs games conducted in multicoloured togs. First staged by Kerry Packer in 1978 and *de rigueur* in the World Cup from 1992. Not all the designers have been blessed with a surfeit of taste, but those blues, yellows, greens and maroons, long considered the last straw by the reactionary, have enlivened the spectacle while further distancing the abbreviated game from its protracted progenitor. For all their commonality of purpose, first-class and limited-overs cricket are fundamentally different: so why not have different outfits? Mind you, the logic in permitting names to adorn shirts in one format but not the other still defies rational analysis.

Quote Unquote

'I hope the Queen was watching.'

Ian Botham, the champion all-rounder, whose stated ambition was to win the World Cup 'in front of 100,000 convicts', after inspiring England to victory over Australia at Sydney in a 1992 group match. During a recent visit by Queen Elizabeth II, Paul Keating, the Australian Prime Minister, had ruffled feathers by slipping an arm around the royal waist.

'We couldn't beat a team of Eskimos.'

Botham on his less-than illustrious successors, 1996.

Reverse Sweep

The most important technical breakthrough for batsmanship in the hundred-odd years since Prince Ranji patented the leg glance. A product of the urgency of the condensed game and a highly effective counter to negative bowling, it requires the striker to turn round in his stance as the bowler delivers, enabling a right-hander, for instance, to sweep a ball pitched outside off-stump. This, in turn, has sired the reverse pull and even the reverse cut. The risks, though, are not to be sniffed at, and even the most adept exponents can be a tad too clever for their own good. Witness Mike Gatting, who effectively lost the 1987 World Cup final with just such a *faux pas*. The advent of the ambidextrous batsman beckons.

Scoring Rates

Runs per over, the acid test and bottom line. Normally depicted on your viewer-friendly television screen as the 'Manhattan', a bar graph tracing the progress of a team's innings over by over. Easier to follow, albeit less instructive, than those infernal intertwining snakes employed to compare rates.

Turner, Alan

Against Sri Lanka at The Oval in 1975, this left-handed, amply eyebrowed Australian opener became the first, and so far only, man in World Cup annals to collect a century before lunch. Given that lunch is now off the menu, this is one record that can be safely wrapped in aspic.

Upsets

Sufficiently scarce to retain every last fragment of their allure and charm, the inclusion of three associate members in 1996 and 1999 has at least multiplied the possibilities. Because physique, speed and stamina play a far more significant part in soccer, where even a draw can dent the Richter scale, the 'other' World Cup has produced countless more surprises. Indeed, with draws a non-option, there have been only three unadulterated shocks, i.e. a non-Test nation beating its supposed betters: Sri Lanka v India in 1979, Zimbabwe v Australia in 1983 and that joyous day for Tariq and his pals against the mighty West Indies in 1996. Kenya may well fancy their chances of trimming another sail or two but don't hold your breath.

Venkataraghavan, Srinivasaraghavan

Has any other sporting figure of world renown ever performed under a moniker comprising two names aggregating 13 syllables? Venkat to all and sundry, this slender, genial offie from Madras featured in the very first World Cup dismissal, catching England's John Jameson while captaining India. He is now revered as the game's foremost umpire (Jamaican Steve Bucknor isn't far behind), and his contribution to the success of this summer's event will be as critical as any. He is honest enough to admit that he doesn't always get it right – an exceedingly rare quality among the higher echelons of his profession – and his mode of execution is nothing if not distinctive. After a considered pause he raises his right arm, bending it at the elbow as if directing traffic. Should he be standing at Chester-le-Street when the Bangladesh batters tackle Glenn McGrath and his fellow Aussies, that is precisely what his function is destined to be.

stock of the era's pre-eminent opener plunged so low.

Thereafter things proceeded as envisaged. England and West Indies won all their group games; Australia and New Zealand, who had recently won their third Gillette Cup and whose seam attack was always going to have the edge over India's, claimed the runners-up spots. Although the gutsy Sri Lankans gave the Australians a run for their money at The Oval, endearing themselves to the Kennington congregation by administering a sound hiding to Lillee and Thomson, England's winter tormentors, both they and the Africans lost all three of their outings. Glenn Turner (171 not out) profited most from the generosity of the African bowlers, then turned the key match in Group A against India with a steadying unbeaten century: not bad for a bloke once pilloried as a blocker of the most stultifying kind.

The semi-finals proved only half as predictable. Lloyd inserted the Kiwis at The Oval, as was his wont, then sat back and watched his pacemen cut them down inside 53 overs. Ian Chappell followed suit at Leeds against the hosts, eager for Lillee and Thomson to do their worst while the pitch was at its greenest and dampest, nerves at their jangliest. Instead, the mayhem was caused by Gary Gilmour, a burly left-armer from Waratah, at 24 the youngest Australian. Touted as the new Alan Davidson, he had already been saddled with an albatross that would peck away at his motivation and contribute to a hasty decline. Although marginally more than a 15-minute hero, foot problems and fragile confidence would snuff his flame within two years. 'Nobody had more talent than that bloke, as much as Gary Sobers,' Greg Chappell would effuse. 'Not many blokes had his natural ball skills. Strong upper body, but very poor legs, ankles not really strong enough for his weight.'

Swinging his deliveries back into an exclusively right-handed top order while maintaining a full length and a brisk pace, Gilmour reeled off his 12 overs unchanged, taking full advantage of the oppressive atmosphere to extract six of the first seven wickets, a dentist pulling molars. Mike Denness, the England captain, tugged his side from 52 for eight to the marginally more respectable quicksand of 93 all out. But the pitch remained anything but trustworthy and England still scented a whiff of hope, all the more so when Arnold, Old and Snow sent Australia spiralling from 17 without loss to 39 for six. Cue Gilmour, some rustic heaves, an unbroken stand of 55 with Doug Walters and a famous Australian victory. 'That was as good an innings as I saw Gary play,' wrote Chappell Minor. 'Sometimes 28 is worth a century.'

That the whole business spanned barely half the allotted 120 overs caused mass harumphing among the press. The flushed, beaming faces of those wrapped up in the tension on the Western Terrace rather suggested the spectators didn't give a flying fig.

Highest Individual Scores

Gary Kirsten	188★	South Africa v UAE, Rawalpindi 1996
Viv Richards	181	West Indies v Sri Lanka, Karachi 1987
Kapil Dev	175★	India v Zimbabwe. Tunbridge Wells 1983
Glenn Turner	171★	New Zealand v East Africa, Birmingham 1975
Andrew Hudson	161	South Africa v Holland, Rawalpindi 1996
Aravinda de Silva	145	Sri Lanka v Kenya, Kandy 1996
David Houghton	142	Zimbabwe v New Zealand, Hyderabad 1987
Viv Richards	138★	West Indies v England, Lord's 1979
Dennis Amiss	137	England v India, Lord's 1975
Sachin Tendulkar	137	India v Sri Lanka, Delhi 1996

★ = *not out batsman*

World Cup Records 1975–96

The Great Match: West Indies v Pakistan
Edgbaston, 11 June

If ever a side had a match trussed up, locked in a vault and beyond rescue Pakistan did here. Chasing 267, West Indies, harried by pace and spin alike and batting brainlessly, had slithered to 166 for eight. 'They drew up the chair for the victory banquet,' reflected the *Daily Telegraph*. Dessert never arrived.

Though deprived of their captain, Asif Iqbal, in hospital for minor surgery, and a promising young all-rounder by the name of Imran Khan, embroiled in exams at Oxford, Pakistan were still eminently capable of running up a serviceable total. Stand-in skipper Majid Khan (60) and Zaheer (31) were close to their velvety peak in a second-wicket stand worth 62, Wasim Raja (58) cut his renowned dash and Mushtaq supplied the spine with a patient, orderly 55. Only canny bowling by knock-kneed Vanburn Holder and lithe Keith Boyce, trusty veterans of the Sunday League both, kept the total down to 266 for seven.

It grew ever more imposing as the West Indies' batsmen took turns to mislay their marbles. Flailing at just about anything, Greenidge, Fredericks and Kallicharran were all gone for 36 as Sarfraz turned in a flattering spell of three for 10 in 22 balls. Lloyd and Kanhai put on 48 but then the latter, easily his side's

Roberts the bruiser: Andy strikes out

most experienced cog, played on to a wide full-toss. The frantic air resumed, Javed Miandad's googly did for Lloyd, and Holder joined wicket-keeper Murray with 101 required. The ninth-wicket liaison was productive, but another 64 were needed when Sarfraz accounted for Holder. Sarfraz was close to the end of his stint but nobody in the Pakistan camp was overly fussed about that.

In hindsight it was critical. Murray found an able ally in Roberts, and the pair of them, alternately biffing and flicking, eroded the target blow by rousing, implacable blow. Between balls, Murray would march down the pitch for a word in Roberts's ear, stiffening his young partner's resolve. So ragged did they run the attack, so repeatedly did Asif Masood over-pitch and feed their rapacious bats, the final over was entrusted to Raja and his hitherto unglimpsed leg-breaks.

It so nearly proved a masterstroke. With five wanted from as many balls, Roberts played

Raja off his hip and dashed for a leg-bye as wicket-keeper Wasim Bari darted from his perch, threw off a glove, gathered the ball and took aim: Roberts was well short but the target was missed, allowing a second run. The fates, it seemed, had already made up their minds. With the field drawn in for the penultimate ball, Roberts pushed the winning single to midwicket and scampered off with a heady smile. Murray was hoisted by his gleeful compatriots from the terraces, 61 and unconquered, the architect-in-chief of one of the most memorable finishes to any cricket match anywhere, of any hue. Perversely, Tom Graveney gave the Man of the Match award to Sarfraz.

Clive Lloyd needed no convincing about the significance – not to say manner – of the win. 'That brought us [together],' he would reflect. 'We were much closer [after that]. We had quite a lot of young players – Viv Richards, David Murray, Kallicharran. That was the start of our great run.' Wasim Bari has much to answer for.

Viv-acious: Viv Richards

Best Batting Averages (50+) *Qualification: 300 runs*

Name	M	I	NO	Runs	HS	Avge	100	50
Saeed Anwar (Pakistan)	6	6	2	329	★83	82.25	–	3
Gary Kirsten (South Africa)	6	6	1	391	★188	78.20	1	1
Graeme Fowler (England)	7	7	2	360	★81	72.00	–	4
Peter Kirsten (South Africa)	8	8	2	410	90	68.33	–	4
Sachin Tendulkar (India)	15	14	2	806	137	67.16	2	6
Viv Richards (West Indies)	23	21	5	1013	181	63.31	3	5
Mark Waugh (Australia)	12	12	2	629	130	62.90	3	2
Glenn Turner (New Zealand)	14	14	4	612	★171	61.20	2	2
Martin Crowe (New Zealand)	21	21	5	880	★100	55.00	1	8
David Boon (Australia)	16	16	1	815	100	54.33	2	5
David Gower (England)	12	11	3	434	130	54.25	1	1
Ramiz Raja (Pakistan)	16	16	3	700	★119	53.84	3	2
Arjuna Ranatunga (Sri Lanka)	25	24	8	835	★88	52.18	–	6
Majid Khan (Pakistan)	7	7	0	359	84	51.28	–	5
Allan Lamb (England)	19	17	4	656	102	50.46	1	3
Brian Lara (West Indies)	14	14	2	602	111	50.16	1	5

The Great Duel: Alvin Kallicharran v Dennis Lillee
The Oval, 14 June

Who says size is everything? Diminutive Alvin, all 5ft next-to-nothing of Guyanese impishness, versus Dennis the Menace, six-foot-plus of prime Australian beef and belligerence. No contest, right? Wrong. Both sides had qualified for the semi-finals, but the edge was far from dulled. Boyce had made short work

Menacing Dennis: Alvin Kallicharran

of the Chappell brothers on a cloud-filled morning, Greenidge, resplendent in powder-blue terrycloth sunhat, had run out Walters with a direct hit and Australia had been skittled for 192. Dennis the Menace was not about to take this lying down.

Max Walker soon got rid of Greenidge, but Roy Fredericks progressed with his usual violent panache until Kalli and his boyishly bobbing black curls replaced his fellow left-hander as the focus of attention, those wristy flourishes evidence of his Asian roots. Nor did it hurt being whooped and hollered on by the vast majority of a full-throated gallery, many bedecked in Rastafarian favours. Creating an atmosphere more redolent of the Kensington Oval than its Kennington cousin, the steel drums and blaring bugles amplified the gleeful surreality.

It wasn't entirely one-way traffic. Having sliced Walker past slip on 15, Kalli forced Lillee square off the back foot but then thick-edged to the third-man boundary. Pirouetting with the jauntiness of a putative Nureyev, he retorted with a pull for four. When the next ball soared above his eyebrows he deposited it with an overhead smash, the impetus forcing his feet clear off the ground. Four boundaries on the trot, 18 off the over, the menace mauled.

The best lay ahead, a pull behind square for six struck with timing, power and a barely suppressed snicker. Another snick past slip coaxed a rueful smile from the victim's pursed lips. Even the moustache was wilting. In a sequence of 10 balls from Lillee, Kalli had helped himself to seven fours and a six. Lillee had the final word, eliciting a mistimed pull with Kalli having collected 62 of his 78 in boundaries. Graciously applauding his conqueror all the way back to the pavilion, here, at last, was the tiger as pussycat. Trinidadians and Jamaicans were united in delight, but no more so than Englishmen.

Results

Group A	P	W	L	Pts
England	3	3	0	12
New Zealand	3	2	1	8
India	3	1	2	4
East Africa	3	0	3	0

Group B	P	W	L	Pts
West Indies	3	3	0	12
Australia	3	2	1	8
Pakistan	3	1	2	4
Sri Lanka	3	0	3	0

Semi-finals

Leeds, 18 June: **England 93** (36.2 overs; Gilmour 6–14); **Australia 94 for six** (28.4 overs; Old 3–29). *Australia won by four wickets.*

The Oval, 18 June: **New Zealand 158** (52.2 overs; Howarth 51, Julien 4–27); **West Indies 159 for five** (40.1 overs; Kallicharran 72, Greenidge 55, Collinge 3–28). *West Indies won by five wickets.*

Putting them through their paces: Dennis Lillee

The Final: West Indies v Australia
Lord's, 21 June

West Indies 291 for eight (Lloyd 102, Kanhai 55, Gilmour 5-48); **Australia 274** (58.4 overs, I Chappell 62, Boyce 4-50). *West Indies won by 17 runs.*

The longest day and, at least until Sri Lanka's applecart-upsetting deeds, the most blissfully euphoric. Twenty-four years on and still the frisson remains. We've already chewed over the significance and ramifications of it all, yet even when analysed in isolation, as a self-contained entity, this match packed sufficient imperishable goods to guarantee a permanent cranny in the memory bank of each and every soul fortunate enough to have borne witness.

Pick a highlight: heaven knows there was no shortage of candidates. Fredericks hooking Lillee for six but dislodging a bail as his back foot slid in the morning dew; the wondrously predatory fielding of Richards and Kallicharran; the look of *mea culpa* writ large across Ian Chappell's fearless visage after the Australian captain had been run out by Richards attempting a third run from a misfield that might conceivably have been within the compass of Valeriy Borzov; the scarcely credible last-wicket stand between Lillee and Thomson that converted a waltz into a cliffhanger; the no-ball that spared Thomson only for the cacophony to drown out Tom Spencer's call, persuading the crowd to think it was all over and invade the arena while the batsmen kept on running. Nevertheless, had a mistimed pull off Lillee by Lloyd, then 26, been held at midwicket by the habitually flaw-free Ross Edwards, both match and occasion would have been fatally undermined.

The godfather: Clive Lloyd

As it was, having seen his first three batsmen go for 50, the purring, pantheresque majesty of the West Indies captain transformed a tussle between bat and ball into something more extraordinary and enduring. Off the field, Lloyd had been grateful indeed for the presence of Kanhai's stabilizing influence, but now he was indebted to the veteran's composure on it. While his greying fellow Guyanan provided the ballast, spending 11½ overs mooching contentedly on 16, the giraffe-like Lloyd underscored his reputation as the first great limited-overs batsman, acquired at Lancashire and now polished to glinting perfection.

Drawing his left foot back as the bowlers approached, thus getting into position early to pull and hook, he surged to 102 off 84 balls as if on castors. All those decades playing second-fiddle to the baggy green caps evaporated in one effortless hook off Lillee into the grandstand. Not since Tommie Smith and

Opening shot: Roy Fredericks

John Carlos had raised their gloved hands on the Olympic podium seven years earlier, it could be argued, had black power been so manifest in an international sporting context.

Even so, West Indies were an iffy 209 for six in the 46th over, and it took a late flurry from Keith Boyce and Bernard Julien to fully capitalize on Lloyd's inroads, pushing the target over the horizon. To date, after all, the highest score to win a 60-over match in England by a pursuing team had been 257. Five run-outs later prophecies were duly fulfilled, but not before the odd sniff of a role reversal, notably when Walters and his skipper were conjoined. And who should bowl Walters but the Windies' most frugal bowler, Clive Hubert Lloyd Esq. Few chaps can ever have won a Man of the Match award by quite so many streets. The winners shared £4,000. Small beer, granted, when compared with the £3m-plus three-year deal Pele had just signed to bulge nets for the New York Cosmos, but nobody was complaining. Yet...

Amid the reams of effusive praise and gratitude, how intriguing to rummage through the files and discover that, although page 20 of the following Monday's *Daily Telegraph* was led by the headline 'Gritty Australians Bow to Lloyd in Thrilling Final', almost as much prominence was accorded the Sunday League clash at Hove ('Tail-ender Waller sees Sussex home'). The paper's correspondent, Michael Melford, also betrayed his disquiet. The game, he noted, 'unfolded at 14 overs an hour amid the clank of cans, the honk of horns and other less-than-tranquil visitations'. Whether the day did the crowd credit, he added, 'is doubtful', citing in particular the theft of Thomson's bat and gloves while claiming the Queenslander had been 'mauled' by spectators. There really is no pleasing some people. Besides, he hadn't seen nothing yet.

England 1979

When the management committee conferred on the eve of the tournament, there was one itch in urgent need of scratching. At Worcester a fortnight previously, Brian Rose, the Somerset captain, in an ingenious if abhorrent attempt to maintain his side's overall scoring rate and thus secure qualification, had declared after one over of a Benson & Hedges Cup zonal game. In so doing, railed *Wisden*, he had 'sacrificed all known cricketing principles'. What was there to stop similarly unscrupulous sorts doing likewise when the same tie-breaker was in force and the stakes were higher? Reminded of the possibilities by Peter May, chairman of the committee and a respected former England captain, all eight competing nations agreed to eschew declarations. Brows were mopped with some vigour.

Some persisted in lamenting the exclusion of South Africa, this at a time when John Vorster, the President who had barred Basil D'Oliveira, had just resigned amid the rancorous fallout over

The Duke of Yorker: Joel Garner

'Muldergate', a slush fund scandal. Otherwise, the main concern among neutrals was the uneven impact of the truce between Kerry Packer and the authorities. Whereas West Indies welcomed back their prodigals, the English and Australian boards, who were in an immeasurably better position to resist forgiveness, elected to retain the exclusion zone. All of which left Lloyd and company heavily fancied to retain their crown.

Pakistan, also at full strength, were expected to mount a stiff challenge, while most partial observers felt that England, galvanized by the bullish Botham and the professorial leadership of Mike Brearley, possessed the wherewithal to go at least one better than they had in 1975 (even if those rumoured plans to unleash Geoff Boycott and his military-medium swingers did fill purists and patriots alike with dread). Canada, runners-up to the fast-emerging Sri Lankans in the ICC Trophy that served as both qualifier and hors d'oeuvres, displaced East Africa as the whipping boys. Still, it was a measure of that residual snootiness that the *Daily Telegraph* preview took second billing to the earth-shattering news that Kenny Sansom had been named captain of the England Under-21 soccer team.

Though nursing scars from a 2-1 defeat in a one-day rubber Down Under during the winter, England brushed aside Australia with some ease in their opening game, the absence of Derek Underwood and Alan Knott proving markedly less detrimental than that of Lillee, Marsh and the Chappells. And guess what? The Poms' most effective bowler turned out to be our chum Boycott, cap affixed to that receding hairline as he lulled two opposition noteworthies into indiscretions, forcing opener Andrew Hilditch to play on and having Kim Hughes, Australia's captain and most strident bat, smearing to midwicket.

It seemed almost fitting when, two days later, John Wayne, the epitome of brute force, gave up the ghost and boarded that great stagecoach in the sky.

The critical match-up in Group A was at Trent Bridge, where the drama of Australia v Pakistan extended over two days thanks to the deluges that had greeted the advent of Thatcherism (and all but sunk the shrimps during the ICC curtain-raiser). In the event, Hilditch's 72 was the highest by either camp but a nonchalant Majid and a busy Asif marshalled the only 250-plus total in the group stages. Supplemented by an incisive spell from the impossibly skinny Sikander during which Hughes and Allan Border were both ejected, Pakistan romped home by 89 runs.

Considerably tighter was England's tilt with Asif's army at Headingley, where the ball reigned yet again: 316 runs trickled from 116 overs, Asif himself alone in reaching 35; as the metronomic Mike Hendrick (12-6-15-4) turned the screw, he still failed to steer his side past the hosts' 165. Canada? Oh, Canada. Hurried out for 45 by England – on second thoughts, 'hurried' is entirely inappropriate since they did manage to grit it out until the 41st over – their Asian-Caribbean collective failed to reach 140 or produce an individual fifty during the tournament.

Group B served up the first tremor. India, already out of contention after failing yet again to beat their peers, were not so much humbled by Sri Lanka as given a lecture in snook-cocking. Making light of the loss of their injured captain, Anura Tennekoon, Sidath Wettimuny, Roy Dias – now the national coach – and Duleep Mendis erected the struts and beams of a more than presentable total. The icing was applied by the tournament's callowest participant, Sudath Pasqual, a 16-year-old schoolboy southpaw; he and Mendis pilfered 52 in seven overs, boosting the booty to 238 for five. Gaekwad, Patel and Vengsarkar, the meat of the Indian order, were flummoxed by Somachandra de Silva's leg-spin and the unlikely lads sauntered home on the Monday by 47 runs, a bold first step on the road to credibility.

Had they been able to tackle West Indies the tournament would

Fabulous Bajan boy: Desmond Haynes

have been much the richer, yet even though three days were set aside for their collision at The Oval, not a ball was propelled. So filthy was the weather during the competition's fortnight run, the fact that only three games spilled over into a second day was considered a miracle of fairly substantial proportions.

The Great Duel: Imran Khan v Ian Botham
Headingley, 16 June

Today's PR machine would probably have billed it as Allah v Godzilla or something similarly tasteless. Teammates and critics with less fondness for the duellists might have opted for Lord Snooty versus the Duke of Daylight Yobbery. They would cross muskets many a time, across courtrooms as well as swards. That nerve-scrambling group match between England and Pakistan, though, constituted the inaugural international confrontation between the era's most inspirational jacks-of-all-trades.

A monument to belligerent self-belief, Botham had hit the ground running. Within three months, on his 21st outing, he would attain the swiftest 'double' – 1,000 runs and 100 wickets – in Test history. The previous summer, against an Imran-less Pakistan, he had become the first man to combine a century and eight wickets in a Test innings. He swung the ball at pace and dismissed balls from his presence with a twang of his smithy's braces. Astonishingly agile for one so beefy, his slip fielding was also the stuff of wonderment. As apt to psyche out as defeat with bat or ball, competitive and utterly professional as he was, he played with the wide-eyed zest of a village enthusiast, detesting inactivity.

In the winter of 1978-79, while Botham was bolstering his rep on official fields, Imran was reinforcing his more calculating mettle in the piratical waters of World Series Cricket. Those subjected to

Khan do: Imran in full flight

the demands of that relentless circus are insistent that it was the most taxing assignment of their careers; the younger guns, as Imran then was, were as one: it hardened them for the jousts ahead.

At Melbourne's VFL Park in December, Imran had shifted Greg Chappell then scattered the WSC Australia tail to level the 'Supertest' series; the following month he helped scuttle WSC West Indies for 67. On pitches that satisfied a fast bowler's every dream, and in highly illustrious company – he invariably went in at No. 8 behind Majid, Amiss, Zaheer, Javed, Asif, Procter and Rice – his bat was by no means embarrassed. As soon as this tournament was over he would be back in Sussex's colours, picking up eight for 81 and 154 not out to demoralize Hampshire.

On a mildly blustery, slightly overcast Leeds morning, Imran had an immediate impact, nabbing Brearley second ball as England stumbled to four for two. Boycott made 18 in an hour and a half, adding 47 with Gooch, and Botham joined Gower for some fleeting jollity but Imran rationed them to two runs an over. All the same, it was Majid's unprepossessing off-breaks that accounted for both English buccaneers.

His beefiness, mark one: Ian Botham

That the total rose from the indefensible to the merely pregnable was due entirely to Willis and that dapper keeper Bob Taylor: previewing their improbable match-winning stand at Edgbaston two summers hence, the ninth-wicket custodians nicked and scraped 43.

Pakistan's reply was even more uncertain: 27 without loss one minute, 34 for six the next. Hendrick reeled in Majid, Sadiq, Mudassar and Haroon in eight balls but Botham inflicted the most grievous wounds, having Zaheer taken at the wicket for three and pinning Javed in front for a duck. When Old did likewise to Raja, Imran joined Asif with 80 required. The target had been whittled down to 51 when Willis did for Asif, but now Bari threw his cussedness into the ring. Brearley brought back Boycott and the talisman did his stuff, dispatching keeper and then Sikander while Imran glowered from the other end, helpless and marooned. Botham was in clover; it would take Imran 13 years to achieve closure.

The Great Match: England v New Zealand
Old Trafford, 20 June

India's haplessness – batsmen too leisurely, seamers too samey, spinners stymied – contrasted starkly with the efficiency of the New Zealanders, who beat them by eight wickets, of Sri Lanka who beat them by nine and of the holders who, despite having to scrap all the way, beat them by 32 runs. The batting mainstay for the Kiwis, once again, had been Turner (146 runs for once out), the most effective bowler Richard Hadlee, a maturing paceman with a quirky habit of taking a backward step at the top of his run (à la Pakistan's Asif Masood): in 33 overs he had given up just 85 runs. He was quick to embellish his CV here, Boycott nicking him to slip in the ninth over, by which juncture England, put in under the bluest skies thus far, had limped to 13. Our old pal McKechnie (pre-Underarm Fracas) lured the cavalier Wayne Larkins into popping a drive to extra-cover, making Mark Burgess's decision to field look like the reasoning of a man equipped with X-ray vision as well as sound guesswork.

Abetted by Gooch, a sedate Brearley repaired some of the damage before cutting one of Jeremy Coney's deceptive dobbers to keeper Warren Lees; when Gower was run out by Lance Cairns' terrific throw, going for a second, the whip hand was firmly in the Kiwis' grasp. For 10 overs Botham and Gooch cast aside the odd shackle, the latter lofting McKechnie for six, but it took Derek Randall's perky 42 not out to ensure respectability as the last three overs went for 25: rare fruits indeed. Trailing an analysis encompassing four maidens and 32 runs, Hadlee had been the thorniest thorn.

Embarking in search of 222, John Wright and Bruce Edgar, lefties both, raised 47 at three an over before Old trapped Edgar. Cue Boycott, suckering Geoff Howarth into missing a full-toss amid a suffocating spell that galled as much as it inspired. Turner prospered awhile but Randall ran out Wright from deep square leg with a typical piece of off-the-cuff chicanery. Willis unglued Turner yet resistance was far from done, Lees and Cairns swatting sixes before Hendrick dug them out.

By now Old was the only home seamer not clutching something tender, and as Botham limped in for the final over, the target had been trimmed to 14 with McKechnie and Gary Troup, the last pair, in attendance. Botham permitted no liberties and England squeezed into the final by nine runs. Gooch was cited Man of the Match for his invaluable 71; though hardly one to bemoan his lot, the worthier candidate was surely the cartwheel-turning, crowd-pleasing, life-affirming Randall, spark plug to the Gods.

Results

Group A	P	W	L	Pts
England	3	3	0	12
Pakistan	3	2	1	8
Australia	3	1	2	4
Canada	3	0	3	0

Group B	P	W	L	No Result	Pts
West Indies	3	2	0	1	10
New Zealand	3	2	1	0	8
Sri Lanka	3	1	1	1	6
India	3	0	3	0	0

Semi-finals

Old Trafford, 20 June: **England 221 for eight** (Gooch 71, Brearley 53); **New Zealand 212 for nine** (Wright 69, Hendrick 3-55). *England won by nine runs.*

The Oval, 20 June: **West Indies 293 for six** (Greenidge 73, Haynes 65, Asif 4-56); **Pakistan 250** (56.2 overs; Zaheer 93, Majid 81, Croft 3-29). *West Indies won by 43 runs.*

Power: Graham Gooch

Patience: Geoff Boycott

Carrying Bat

(No opening batsman has carried his bat in a World Cup match in the traditional sense, i.e. left not out in an all-out team total. The following performances are all occasions where an opener remained not out with a score of 100 or more.)

Gary Kirsten	188★	South Africa v UAE, Rawalpindi 1996
Glenn Turner	171★	New Zealand v East Africa, Birmingham 1975
Sachin Tendulkar	127★	India v Kenya, Cuttack 1996
Geoff Marsh	126★	Australia v New Zealand, Chandigarh 1987
Ramiz Raja	119★	Pakistan v New Zealand, Christchurch 1992
Andy Flower	115★	Zimbabwe v Sri Lanka, New Plymouth 1992
Glenn Turner	114★	New Zealand, v India, Manchester 1975
Gordon Greenidge	106★	West Indies v India, Birmingham 1979
Gordon Greenidge	105★	West Indies v Zimbabwe, Worcester 1983
Sunil Gavaskar	103★	India v New Zealand, Nagpur 1987
Ramiz Raja	102★	Pakistan v West Indies, Melbourne 1992

The Final: West Indies v England
Lord's, 23 June

West Indies 286 for nine (Richards 138 not out, King 86); **England 194** (51 overs; Brearley 64, Boycott 57, Garner 5–38). *West Indies won by 92 runs.*

While Majid and Zaheer were stroking 166 in 36 overs in The Oval semi-final there was every chance that Clive Lloyd and his cohorts would fail to take their preordained place at Lord's. Instead, in the space of a dozen deliveries, a snorting Colin Croft prised out both, together with Javed Miandad, allowing the bookies to breathe anew. As they scanned a batting order that had chalked up a competition-record 293 for six against an attack that had confined their standard-bearers to 165, England supporters had no reason to anticipate anything other than a man-sized hammering.

For all that, it was the Roberts-Croft-Holding-Garner hit squad that most disconcerted the home selectors, hence their nomination of seven batsmen. The downside to this was that Brearley would be obliged to deploy a dozen overs from Boycott, Gooch and Larkins. True, Boycott had been uncannily useful, but the thoughts of what havoc Richards, Greenidge, Kallicharran and Lloyd might wreak were never distant once it dawned that the weather gods were in a beneficent frame of mind.

King for a day: Collis King

Initially, the 'fifth bowler' dilemma appeared unlikely to arise. Achieving copious aerial movement once Brearley had opted to field, Hendrick and Botham made Greenidge and Desmond Haynes chisel out every run before Randall outdashed Greenidge, running him out with an underarm effort as startling as it was legitimate. Hendrick bowled Kallicharran round his legs and snaffled Haynes at slip off Old, who later intercepted a return drive from Lloyd – 99 for four and the citadel showing encouraging signs of crumbling.

Helmets were now *de rigueur* but Richards disdained such insults to his manhood. Inspired, perhaps, by the void created by Muhammad Ali's latest – and reportedly irrevocable – vow to hang up his gumshield, he came out jabbing and moving, respectful of Phil Edmonds's slow and cunning left-arm variations, but nothing else. Shimmying across his stumps as the seamers uncoiled, he was soon clipping decent deliveries outside off and plonking them against the midwicket hoardings. Richie Benaud's

Pulling his weight: Viv Richards

on-air responses captured the rapture. A haughty flick off Hendrick – 'That's arrogance at its best.' A swept six into the Tavern off Gooch – 'There's, er, a certain amount of contempt in that.' A return drive compelling Hendrick to duck frantically in his follow-through – 'Very wise, very wise indeed.'

Remarkable as it may seem, however, Richards, though ultimately awarded the Man of the Match medal, was not England's torturer-in-chief. Step forward Collis King, a slim and supple Barbadian all-rounder, who, scenting his 15 minutes of fame, grabbed them with an innings as carefree as it was serene. Of the 139 runs ransacked by the fifth-wicket alliance in an hour and a quarter, King donated 86, the timing of his driving often leaving his partner looking comparatively pedestrian; 86 also happened to be the precise number of runs conceded by Messrs Boycott, Gooch and Larkins as they collaborated on their grubby dozen overs.

At tea, on paper, England were in with half a sniff. Boycott and Brearley had yet to be parted, the opening stand deep into three figures. In reality such optimism was misplaced. The Yorkshireman had spent 17 overs reaching double figures; inevitably, the onus on their successors to pick up the slack proved unfeasible. When King caught Brearley 158 were wanted off 22 overs; less than an hour had elapsed when Croft bowled Hendrick, putting the patients, unravelled by Garner's yorkers, out of their misery. From St John's Wood to St Kitts, the rum punches flowed well into the wee small hours. Those rastaman vibrations were on the house.

England 1983

On the opening day at The Oval, a born-and-bred South African by the name of Lamb devoured every juicy morsel ladled up by a New Zealand attack that, aside from the ever-dependable Hadlee, laid on 296 runs in 48 overs. Meanwhile, at Swansea, Pakistan (338 for five) and Sri Lanka (288 for nine) aggregated 626 runs in a day. After all the seam-dominated fare of previous tournaments, was the imbalance receding? Affirmative.

Twenty-four qualifying games would furnish just eight completed innings that failed to reach 200, an appreciably more encouraging ratio than those of 1975 (11 in 12) or 1979 (eight in 12). Given that the elements, so savage in May, had relented for a menu comprising almost twice as many items – 27 games compressed into 17 days – one might have imagined the gates would increase in direct proportion. In fact, they rose by 'only' 76 per cent, from 132,000 to 232,000 (the 1975 event, rewarded with more clement weather than its successor, brought in 158,000). By the same token, with several of the non-Test venues restricted by four-figure capacities, and the senior stages themselves more Old Vic than National Theatre, it would have been unrealistic to demand many more.

Not until the tournament went further afield could its commercial possibilities be fully realized. 'The wealthier countries can sustain the future of the World Cup: India, indeed, could guarantee its solvency,' advocated Arlott, no longer decorating the airwaves with that inimitable Hampshire burr but still tuned into practical realities. 'For British spectators, though, this may be the last chance to enjoy it for

Sweeping success: David Gower

some time to come.' The ICC recognized as much when its constituents met for a post-final chinwag and invited tenders from putative alternative hosts.

The England of 1983 wasn't that marked an advance on the 1979 model. Lester Piggott had just won his ninth Derby, Maggie Thatcher retained the keys to 10 Downing Street the day after Lamb's frolic, and the nation's most devoted chairbound umpires, line judges and ball persons were limbering up for their cherished summer ritual:

riling John 'Superbrat' McEnroe at Wimbledon. The World Cup, on the other hand, was growing up. It was still limited to eight participants: Zimbabwe made their debut after winning the 1982 ICC Trophy, while Sri Lanka, now part of the Test clan, qualified as of right. In other respects, however, everything was bigger and better, not to say fairer. Doubling the frequency of group fixtures also permitted each combatant two bites at each of its fellow group members, thus diminishing the potential impact of pluvial interference. What ensued was the most vibrant World Cup yet.

The four-handed overture even threw up a brace of genuine gobsmackers. At Trent Bridge, Zimbabwe deflated the baggy green caps with less difficulty than the 13-run margin would infer. Hats were doffed to their captain Duncan Fletcher, once a professional with Rishton in the Lancashire League and later to coach Glamorgan to a rare county championship pennant, who capped an unconquered 69 against the ageing Lillee and Thomson by sending back the first four Australians to boot. Hughes, his opposite number, took it on the chin, pronouncing that his side had been 'outplayed'. The absence of Greg Chappell, who'd ricked his neck in Sri Lanka, was glossed over – for now. At Old Trafford, India, emboldened by a recent piece of effrontery against the same opponents in Berbice, downed the holders to record their first World Cup triumph against taxing opposition. Asked to bat on a moist surface, they lurched to 141 for five whereupon Yashpal Sharma's 89 spirited them to 262 for eight, their tallest 60-over score. Closing a truncated day on 67 for two, the holders lost the next seven wickets for 81 whereupon Garner and Roberts outdid Murray and Roberts, making 71 for the last wicket before Kirmani stumped Garner, consigning West Indies to their first reversal in 11 World Cup matches.

Gower was at his most felicitous as England ran Group A, averaging five runs an over. By the time they sustained their sole defeat, to New Zealand – who'd repeatedly bettered them during the winter – they had already seen off each of their rivals. Gooch, banned for touring South Africa alongside various has-beens and never-weres, was scarcely missed. The Kiwis had seemed a good bet to join them in the last four when they beat Pakistan at Edgbaston after Hadlee and Cairns had sent Imran's men spinning to nought for three. But that theory wobbled in a three-wicket upending at Derby by Sri Lanka, now coached by Sir Gary Sobers and evidently feeling the benefits. Sobers compared the passion for the game on the island with that in the Caribbean: founded on such passion, the possibilities appeared endless.

Back at Trent Bridge for the decider, Zaheer and Imran added 147 at two a minute without being parted as Pakistan stacked up a more than serviceable 261 for three. Even though the injured Imran was wearing only his batting hat, no Kiwi was able to emulate that sort of command. Still Martin Crowe and captain Geoff Howarth chipped in fruitfully and Coney dominated a 59-run ninth-wicket liaison with John Bracewell at 12 an over. Thirteen wanted off the last six balls, 12 as Coney turned for a second from Sarfraz's first delivery; Imran threw him out. Once all the columns had been totted and the long divisions completed, Pakistan had nudged through to the next stage by eight-hundredths of a run.

The champions lost no time in recovering their brio: Greenidge, Haynes and Richards did much as they pleased, Malcolm Marshall introduced himself as a more than able heir to Croft, and Winston Davis duffed up the Aussies. The chief features of Group B were the eclipse of Australia, and India's coming of age. Hughes did oversee victory over India, and by a whopping 162 runs at that as Trevor 'Mr Underarm' Chappell became the first and least likely product of that notable clan to collect a World Cup century. From there, though, it was bluey after bluey, not least when, having forged an impressive 273 for six in the return against Lloyd's boys, Australia went down with more than two overs to spare, the reliance on Chappell as fifth bowler ill-conceived and duly punished. India sealed the green caps' fate – and their own passage – with a 118-run cruise at Chelmsford: their inferior scoring-rate meant that the reverse outcome would have spared the Australians.

Rogered: India's Roger Binny takes a return catch to send back Graham Yallop as Australia crash out at Chelmsford

The Great Match: India v Zimbabwe
Tunbridge Wells, 18 June

Should Bollywood ever commission a biopic of Errol Flynn, it would need look no further than Kapil Dev to play the starring role. A lean, handsome, 'tache-twirling all-rounder with flashing eyes and dashing sensibilities, here was Indian cricket's first true heart-throb. He was also his country's first bona fide fast bowler. In time he would establish the extant benchmark of 434 Test wickets. All the same, it was with the bat that he thrilled. Ringed by rhododendrons on England's prettiest county ground, it was that low-slung, smoothly swung blade that saved his country from the blushes endured by Australia.

'The most remarkable day of my life,' he would testify in his autobiography, published four springs later. How could he have known that, in 1990, he would avert the follow-on in a Test in the grandest of manners when, with only an inefficient No. 11 for company, he shelled the Lord's extremities with four consecutive sixes? For sheer nerve that took the biscuit; this was different. He was livid.

Hounded by a damp bitch of a pitch, hustled by Peter Rawson and Kevin Curran (soon to dig up an Irish grandmother in a forlorn attempt to represent England), India had slumped to nine for four when their captain was summoned. Having already decided to bat before he won the toss – he wanted a total that would improve his 66-1 outsiders' run-rate regardless of how their counterparts fared – he was already in severe debt. 'I was in a trance-like state,' he would recall. Sharma's exit at 17 did nothing to alleviate it.

As the surface dried and withdrew its horns, Kapil progressed gingerly: batting out the full 60 overs was the extent of his ambition. Come lunch he was still fuming, though less with his own misdemeanour than those of his charges. 'When I walked into the dressing-room I saw everyone trooping out. A glass of water had been left next to my chair. It [was] usually the custom for one of the reserves to bring the not-out batsmen's lunch to the dressing-room [but] there was no sign of my lunch. I had to walk up to the dining-room. My teammates knew I could not possibly yell at them in public. I appreciated their plan and their sense of humour in leaving only that glass of water, indicating I should cool down.'

Thereafter he transferred his ire to the bowlers. A mishit pull off Curran flew for six, prompting the bowler to hurl a terse rejoinder. Dander up, Kapil dared him to venture another bouncer. Bait swallowed, a hook sailed out of the ground. Kapil held out his bat and pointedly proffered it to Curran, 'From a trance I had progressed to a daze.'

At 140 for eight India had every prospect of acquiring the 150 Kapil felt imperative if his own bowlers were to have something to defend with a smidgin of positivism. The fun, though, had only just begun. Finding a sturdy aide in Syed Kirmani, exemplary wicket-keeper and team-man but best known as international cricket's first slaphead, Kapil orchestrated, conducted and played lead violin in an unbroken ninth-wicket stand worth 126 off 16 overs. In all he hit 16 fours in addition to six sixes, an unbeaten 175 unseating Turner as keeper of the competition-best.

Not that the Africans bowed meekly – anything but. At 113 for six they were going down for the third time, but Curran had a score to settle, and although Kapil remained close to unhittable, he shook the Indians with a rambunctious 73. Only when he was caught in the 56th over, with Zimbabwe 37 short at 230 for nine, could Kapil relax. The skipper had the final word, too, seeing off John Traicos, the last man, with three overs gone a-begging.

Curran and his buddies had demonstrated that they were more than mere one-shock wonders; had Curran and Graeme Hick not been so impatient, indeed, they would have been consorting regularly with the big boys appreciably earlier than 1991, when they were finally promoted to full ICC membership. As for the victors... 'I had, by the grace of God, infused a new enthusiasm to our campaign,' their captain would write. History was not about to quibble.

Giant-killer: Duncan Fletcher

Daredevil: Kapil Dev

Highest Partnerships (any wicket)

207 (3rd) **Mark Waugh & Steve Waugh**, Australia v Kenya, Visakhapat 1996

195★ (3rd) **Gordon Greenidge & Larry Gomes**, West Indies v Zimbabwe, Worcester 1983

186 (1st) **Alan Hudson & Gary Kirsten**, South Africa v Holland, Rawalpindi 1996

184 (3rd) **Asanka Gurusinha & Aravinda de Silva**, Sri Lanka v Kenya, Kandy 1996

182 (1st) **Rick McCosker & Alan Turner**, Australia v Sri Lanka, The Oval 1975

182 (3rd) **Desmond Haynes & Viv Richards**, West Indies v Sri Lanka, Karachi 1987

176 (2nd) **Dennis Amiss & Keith Fletcher**, England v India, Lord's 1975

175 (1st) **Desmond Haynes & Brian Lara**, West Indies v Pakistan, Melbourne 1992

(West Indies reached 221 for no wicket, but Lara retired hurt at 175)

175 (3rd) **Sachin Tendulkar & Mohammad Azharuddin**, India v Sri Lanka, Delhi 1996

172★ (1st) **Desmond Haynes & Faoud Bacchus**, West Indies v Zimbabwe, Birmingham 1983

172 (3rd) **Asanka Gurusinha & Aravinda de Silva**, Sri Lanka v Zimbabwe, Colombo 1996

The Great Duel: Zaheer Abbas v Viv Richards
The Oval, 22 June

'I juggled the bowlers. Of course I did. I moved the field around, trying to cut off their favourite shots. It made no difference at all. "Zed" is predominantly an off-side player and he continually stepped away to beat the ball through the cover region, even towards the long boundary. At one point I posted three fielders on that boundary line, yet in a single over he smashed three fours there without one of the fielders getting within five yards of the ball.'

There were not that many occasions during his success-studded career when Mike Gatting felt impotent. In early July, however, the pre-eminent English captain of his generation would experience that

In his pomp: Viv Richards

very sensation. Regaling Lord's on Gloucestershire's behalf in a Sunday League pitch-and-bash, Zaheer's response to Middlesex's 40-over high of 270 was to mastermind a cascade of 100 runs in the final 10 overs, pocketing the points with four balls to spare. 'If I had been sitting in the stands as a neutral observer, I am quite sure I would have loved every brilliant shot of it,' mused Gatting of Zaheer's unbeaten century. 'As it was, my only feeling was one of relief when the agony stopped – rather like stepping out of a dentist's chair.'

Gatting was mistaken in one respect. It is exceedingly doubtful whether 'Zed' ever 'smashed' a ball. Caressed, stroked, glanced, eased – yes, but brutalized? From the finest purveyor of – as his 'ghost' David Foot so elegantly put it – 'the receding art of pure batsmanship'? That, surely, was the province of King Viv. In Lahore the previous December this insatiable Pakistani, now preferring contacts to spectacles, had joined the exclusive 'Hundred Hundreds' club; at 35 he was the team's elder statesman, held in awe. Inclined to introspection, he was accepted as a man apart, a man to envy and cherish but never disturb. 'He doesn't like fielding too much,' Foot was apprised by a dressing-room cohabitant, 'and we understand that.'

The Zed-Viv debate was always going to be intrinsic to the outcome of The Oval semi-final. Pakistan's champion had veered between the sublime and the blushworthy: 82 and 15 in the two meetings with Sri Lanka, 83 not out and 0 against England, 0 and 103 not out against New Zealand. After an iffy start, Richards had imposed himself as only he could, gleaning Man of the Match awards against India and Australia. That said, he hadn't touched wood at all in the previous match: openers Haynes and Faoud Bacchus had scampered past Zimbabwe's 171 on their tod.

Javed's flu was a grave setback for Pakistan, who sneezed early on a true pitch, shipping Mudassar and Ijaz with 34 on the board. Zaheer came in to abet Mohsin, the youth whose refined strokeplay so mirrored his own, and who the previous July had become the first double-centurian in a Lord's Test since 1949. Boundaries, admittedly, were at a premium – the entire innings would contain but two – yet the pair grew in assurance and substance, seeing off Garner and Holding; the 50 stand came, a taster, it seemed, for untold riches. The West Indies' fifth bowler was the usual mix 'n' match: Larry Gomes and Richards, each offering a mix of genteel spin and unobtrusive seam. Eyes lit up. In the last over of the morning, Zaheer, on 30, swanned out to Gomes and contrived, somehow, to play on; visions of a workable total vanished with him. Mohsin hung around, but nobody else reach 20.

Though he was the next highest scorer with 17, Imran was still constrained from turning his arm over; the holders hardly broke sweat. When Qadir bowled Haynes at 56, Richards and Gomes linked up once more. Adding 132, they polished off the task with fully 11 overs remaining, Richards, as ever, leading the way, leaving Zaheer to regret his flash of impurity.

Results

Group A				
	P	**W**	**L**	**Pts**	**Av runs/over**
England	6	5	1	20	4.67
Pakistan	6	3	3	12	4.01
New Zealand	6	3	3	12	3.93
Sri Lanka	6	1	5	4	3.75

Group B				
	P	**W**	**L**	**Pts**	**Av runs/over**
West Indies	6	5	1	20	4.31
India	6	4	2	16	3.87
Australia	6	2	4	8	3.81
Zimbabwe	6	1	5	4	3.49

Semi-finals

Old Trafford, 22 June: **England 213** (Kapil 3–35); **India 217 for four** (54.4 overs; Sharma 61, Patil 51 not out). *India won by six wickets.*

The Oval, 22 June: **Pakistan 184 for eight** (Mohsin 70, Marshall 3-28); **West Indies 188 for two** (48.4 overs; Richards 80 not out, Gomes 50 not out). *West Indies won by eight wickets.*

White knight: Zaheer Abbas

Jimmy's riddle: Mohinder Arnarnath traps Michael Holding to seal India's 1983 triumph

The Final: India v West Indies
Lord's, 25 June

India 183 (54.4 overs; Roberts 3-32); **West Indies 140** (52 overs; Amarnath 3-12, Madan Lal 3-31). *India won by 43 runs.*

'As a team we had come to believe we were invincible. It was unthinkable as far as I and some others were concerned that we could ever lose anything important.' Thus admitted Malcolm Marshall. He also conceded that West Indies of 1983 carried 'a decidedly complacent air'. Which explains why the young man who would grow up to be the most prolific bowler ever to spring from the Caribbean apportioned his winner's bonus *before* the final, ordering a spanking new BMW. On reflection, he would be unable to comprehend such 'arrogance and stupidity'.

India's comfortable defeat of England in the Manchester semi-final should have served as sufficient forewarning. On a pitch bearing more than a passing resemblance to the low, slow strips of Bombay and Calcutta, Kapil and his band of seemingly meek medium-paced all-rounders locked the hosts in chains and threw away the key. None, moreover, was meaner than Mohinder Amarnath, Jimmy to one and all, scourge of Gatting and Gower. On a Lord's surface that also declined to allow the ball to come on to the bat with any urgency, not to mention affording constant movement off the seam, the strokemeisters were always going to struggle.

Backed extravagantly by the bookies, Lloyd was true to form, calling correctly on a sunkissed morning and inviting India to bat. Roberts had had Gavaskar caught behind in his third over when Kris Srikkanth availed us of his verve as well as his tics, pinging Holding for six and pranging the pavilion rails, then nodding to himself in sheepish self-admiration. Amarnath helped add 57 for the second wicket but 90 for two dwindled to 130 for seven as Roberts, Holding, Garner and Marshall, the most fearsome of the foursomes to wield the seam for West Indies in World Cup finals, defied defiance. Bouncers or no, the horsemen retained that apocalyptic air.

Only by dint of some late manoeuvrings from messrs nine, ten and jack did the rate scrape above three an over, the innings fading away with 32 balls unbowled. As his downcast troops prepared to take the field, Kapil spelled out his philosophy: 'We have nothing to lose. Nobody expected us to be here. It is only a matter of three hours from now. Throw yourselves at the ball and try.' And so they jolly well did, though the less said about the first half of West Indies' riposte the better.

It started brightly enough. Haynes soon lost Greenidge, bowled shouldering arms to an attempted outswinger from the patka-clad Sandhu, whereupon he and Richards took the score to 50 without further ado or alarm. Richards, indeed, appeared to be in the mood for a solo demolition until Kapil, judging his run immaculately as the ball swirled over his shoulder, clung on to a top-edged pull that took an eternity to descend. 'I was being driven by some kind of a force which I cannot define,' explained the catcher. Whereafter all hell broke loose.

Matthew Engel, for whom Richards had been playing a game 'somewhere between cricket and a sophisticated form of clock golf', pithily enumerated the litany of sins for *Guardian* readers, 'Greenidge did not play a ball he should have done and was bowled; Gomes and Bacchus made the reverse mistake; Lloyd, in pain after aggravating his groin injury, and Haynes both mis-drove.'

Fifty for one had lurched to 76 for six. Hope returned as Jeff Dujon, quite the coolest of dudes and on his day every bit as graceful as Zaheer, put on 43 with Marshall: 64 to get and oodles of overs to get 'em. Then Dujon made to leave one from Amarnath only to see the ball cannon from bat into stumps: the slap of glove on soil was eloquence itself. Holding and Garner held on for half an hour before Amarnath trapped the Jamaican, nailing down Mike Brearley's Man of the Match citation. Even as the crowd burst its banks and swamped the arena, Holding was still rooted to the spot, transfixed in disbelief.

Smiles better: Kapil Dev and Mohinder Arnarnath share the fruits

Up in the press box, words were being consumed. 'If the same personnel could be reassembled another 50 times, India probably would not win again,' contended Engel. 'It is a bit like the infinite number of monkeys at an infinite number of typewriters eventually writing *Hamlet*. And there were an infinite number of us typewriter-types feeling like monkeys.'

Marshall returned to Hampshire 'a chastened man'; he was not alone. 'The world was laughing at us,' he would recount. As corks popped across the pavilion stairwell, Lloyd, weary and dumbfounded, confronted his acolytes and dropped the day's second bomb. 'I have had enough,' the *pater familias* announced as his hushed losers bowed their heads. 'Somebody else can take over.' In the event he would recant, and guide them to ever more rarefied heights, but that evening, as far as Marshall and his pals were concerned, an era had been terminated. With extreme prejudice. West Indies have never been a one-day force since.

For the Indians, conversely, a new age had received the green light. Here were 11 heroes to exalt. They had shown that there was a branch of the game in which the nation's best could tilt at windmills and prevail. Reminded of another breakthrough that spring – Richard Attenborough's *Gandhi* had scooped an armful of Oscars – cricket's largest, most passionate audience could walk tall, wooed anew.

India & Pakistan 1987

And lo, in the fullness of time, it came to pass that the World Cup stretched its legs, swam oceans, and resurfaced with a brand new face. Shorter daylight hours necessitated the adoption of 50-over ties, already the norm in limited-overs internationals outside Blighty, which in turn confined bowlers to 10 apiece. Balls rising above shoulders were formally enshrined as wides, neutral umpires were introduced, ditto fines for tardy over-rates. What ensued was an event fit for a continent rather than an island.

After three tournaments and an investment in excess of £1m, Prudential had put a damper on the 1983 final by announcing that enough was enough. Still, with the surplus distributed among the ICC's full and associate members also having surpassed the magic million, the queue for successors was extensive. So, too, was the clamour to host the next bash. When the subcontinent got the nod, Reliance won the right to affix its name to the trophy while all manner of 'official suppliers' flocked to the cause, from Bank of Baroda and couriers DHL to Maheshwari Nutrition (crisps) and Zandu (pain balm). Logistics would always make cosy Britain the least problematic setting but change was patently essential if the bulk of the iceberg was ever to reveal itself.

There were, of course, certain inherent niggles. One correspondent with a keen grasp of geography likened it to staging the soccer World Cup across Europe, an undertaking never contemplated, much less attempted. For one four-match sequence the Sri Lankans were obliged to charge from northern Pakistan to central India, back to Pakistan then off again to India, each trip a sapping two-day hike. The one blatant gaffe was a ruling stipulating that group matches could extend into a second day only if no play whatsoever was possible on the first; mercifully, only one, Australia v New Zealand, was affected by the weather – and that was reduced to 30 overs per side. So the nonsense, however fortuitously, remained strictly theoretical nonsense. For their valiance in taking on such a forbidding assignment, none the less, the organizing committee, emanating as they did from nations habitually at each other's throats, eminently deserved a leg-up from the fates.

Concern was expressed about the 9 a.m. starts. Would the morning dew be the handicap it invariably was for sides batting first in the NatWest Trophy final? Happily, such vexations proved unfounded: in more than two-thirds of the fixtures the team batting first prevailed. So much for the received wisdom about the desirability of knowing the exact nature of the target. Better still, spin, at last, had found a conducive environment. Nevertheless, even though Qadir, Maninder Singh, Dipak Patel, Roger Harper, Eddie Hemmings and dear old John Traicos did more than their share of enmeshing, even though the two most catalytic dismissals were the doing of a twirler – and a part-time one at that – the leading wicket-takers, Craig McDermott (18) and Imran (17), were both of the bone-splintering variety. It was this sense of balance that made the fourth World Cup the most satisfactory and satisfying yet.

It began not with one bang but four. In Hyderabad, Zimbabwe and Sri Lanka came within four and 16 runs respectively of dumping New Zealand and Pakistan on their backsides; in Gujranwala, England nipped West Indies by two wickets with three balls to spare as Lamb went on the slaughter and Courtney Walsh's final two overs cost 31; in Madras, to top even that, India and Australia scripted the closest World Cup match to date (of which more anon). After the largely one-sided amateur dramatics of past tourneys, a start as auspicious as this would take some living up to. Anticlimax, happily, proved minimal.

With the format unaltered, the outcome of the preliminaries, by and large, adhered to the form book. Triumphant in both the Perth Challenge and the World Series Cup in Australia the previous winter, England had been stung by the voluntary withdrawals of Botham and Gower, yet still qualified with plenty in hand, mood lightened when news came that the horrendously unprecedented storms back home had spared their kith and kin. Their reversals were both inflicted by Pakistan, 2–1 favourites and eventual Group B winners, whose 18-run win in Rawalpindi saw Qadir reacquaint himself with the

Showing a leg: Abdul Qadir

twitchy bats he had mesmerised during the northern hemisphere summer – with predictable results. While Zaheer may have departed, the similarly demure Salim Malik had arrived, as had Wasim Akram, an Imran protégé, fast-evolving into the world's sprightliest left-armer and a hefty humptier to boot. And Javed was still jutting and jabbing.

In Lahore, West Indies too were victimized by Qadir, albeit not in the manner accustomed. Now led by Richards in flesh as well as spirit, they had racked up a new one-day zenith of 360 for four against Sri Lanka, who lacked the bowling resources to match their vibrant strokemakers and had more or less shot their bolt. At his most merciless that day, Richards mellowed thereafter, a god discovering vincibility; more significant even than Walsh's lapses were the absences of Greenidge (crocked knee), Holding (retired), Garner and Marshall (unavailable); cynics, unsurprisingly, linked the withdrawal of the last two to the no-bouncer regulation, although Garner did announce his retirement a month later. Nor should it be forgotten that, the previous winter, Richards's men had turned up for both of Australia's limited-overs showpieces and failed to reach the final stages of either. Beyond all that, though, it was hard to suppress the suspicion that the desire, in the shorter game if not the more demanding variant, had petered out.

Group A would have been vastly more competitive had Hadlee, forgivably fatigued, not pulled out after spearheading Nottinghamshire's championship triumph with the shire's first 1,000 runs-100 wickets double in two decades. Crowe's growing mastery of all facets of batsmanship more than compensated for the retirements of Coney and Edgar, but no Hadlee? No comment.

The holders did their supporters' bidding and more, scoring at a sprightlier rate than any and easing into the last four with a bravura bordering on the cocksure. In the final preliminary against the Kiwis, bouffant-haired seamer Chetan Sharma, unfazed by the number of brows his action furrowed, gathered the World Cup's first hat-trick, all clean bowled, whereupon a target of 222 was knocked off at seven an over. Eyebrows arched even higher when Gavaskar, a turbo-charged mollusc a dozen light years earlier, clattered Ewan Chatfield for six, six, four, four off consecutive deliveries en route to a century off 85 balls – his first in 106 limited-overs internationals. At the other end was the young pretender, Mohammad Azharuddin, building on the blend of artistry and majesty he had unveiled against England in 1984-85, when he blessed each of his first three Tests with a century.

In reaching the knockout stage for the first time since 1975, Australia were scarcely less impressive, albeit unexpectedly so. Setting great store by proper acclimatization and preparation (they'd spent two weeks beforehand adjusting in Madras), if the bowling appeared at that point to lack a focus, a leader, no matter. Smarting from South African defections and successive Ashes drubbings, the determination and all-for-oneness was apparent from the way they buzzed in the field under Border, a captain leading by deed and dedication. Coach Bob Simpson had imposed a strenuous practice regime, interminable catching drills the house speciality; the benefits were soon apparent. The quality of batting, moreover, was not that far short of India's, the acquisitive solidity of openers Geoff Marsh and David Boon prefacing a punchy array led by Dean Jones, in many eyes the condensed form's deftest run manufacturer. There was also a youngster named Steve Waugh, whose burgeoning value as a middle-order hustler was matched by subtle manipulation of the seam. Narrow winners of both bouts with their antipodean cousins, their sole defeat, to India, came in the wake of an opening trio of successes that all but guaranteed progress.

The one downbeat note was struck when a tricky pitch at Cuttack prevented the sort of score required to supersede India's frolicsome run-rate and thus avoid Pakistan in the next phase. Their 266 was still more than sufficient, mind, to facilitate a stroll past Zimbabwe, the ICC champions, whose grit earned them many friends and whose wicket-keeper, David Houghton, could fairly lay claim to the outstanding innings of the tournament. In that coruscating collision with the Kiwis he swept to 141 off 138 balls after his first seven colleagues had cobbled together 30 between them.

Best Bowling Figures		
Winston Davis	7-51	West Indies v Australia, Leeds 1983
Gary Gilmour	6-14	Australia v England, Leeds 1975
Ken Macleay	6-39	Australia v India, Nottingham 1983
Alan Hurst	5-21	Australia v Canada, Birmingham 1979
Paul Strang	5-21	Zimbabwe v Kenya, Patna 1996
Richard Hadlee	5-25	New Zealand v Sri Lanka, Bristol 1983
Shaukat Dukanwala	5-29	UAE v Holland, Lahore 1996
Asantha De Mel	5-32	Sri Lanka v New Zealand, Derby 1983
Dennis Lillee	5-34	Australia v Pakistan, Leeds 1975
Damien Fleming	5-36	Australia v India, Bombay 1996

World Cup Records 1975-96

The Great Match: India v Australia
Madras, 9 October

Barely a year earlier they'd locked antlers on the same Chepauk expanse, scrapping and staggering their way to history's second tied Test. While comparisons of the two are idiotic as well as odious, the replay was no less remorseless in the way it plucked and stretched the nerve-ends.

Put in Australia marched to 174 for one as Marsh stole his third one-day century off Indian bowling and Jones pierced the field with customary suss and sassiness. All the signs pointed to an uncatchable target, but captain Kapil and Manoj Prabhakar kept a tight rein on the middle order, and Border had to settle for 270 for six. It would have been two fewer had not Hanif Mohammad, for two decades the fulcrum of the Pakistan batting and now employed as match adjudicator, subsequently ruled that one blow by Jones was worth six, not the originally-signalled four.

Giving their all: Australia's David Boon pulls against India (above) while Steve Waugh survives an attempted run out (top)

At first, India reacted as if it were a doddle. Gavaskar (37 off 32 balls) and Srikkanth (70 off 83) galloped out of the blocks, then Navjot Sidhu, the slender Sikh debutant, picked up the baton with 73 off 79 balls, including a quintet of sixes; McDermott's first four overs disappeared for 31. His second spell was as dynamic as the first had been listless: Sidhu and Azharuddin had their timbers shivered, Dilip Vengsarkar was pouched by Jones and the troublesome Ravi Shastri sent back via a return catch – four wickets in six overs. Then the irrepressible Jones ran out Roger Binny and Border did likewise for Prabhakar.

As a consequence, 207 for two had dwindled to 265 for nine when Border entrusted Waugh with the final over. Six to get, and four safely gathered before Waugh ripped out the last man's off-stump. That the chap in question happened to be Maninder, who succumbed to the fifth ball, just as he had done in the final over to seal the tied Test, served merely to accentuate the rush of *déjà vu*.

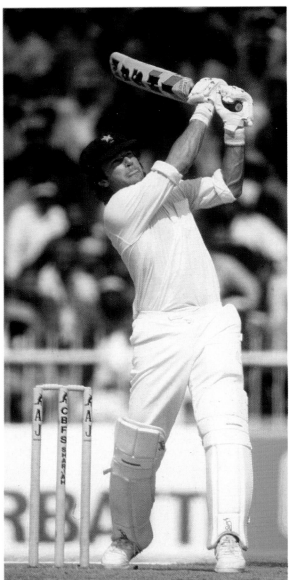

Ginger and Spice: Craig McDermott (left) and Imran Khan (right)

The Great Duel: Imran Khan v Craig McDermott
Lahore, 4 November

The stage was set, lines rehearsed, chickens counted. This was Imran's farewell to the Gadaffi Stadium, the ground where his gifts were nurtured. Pakistan's captain had announced that the tournament would be his final act as an international cricketer. To fall now, to lose a semi-final for the third time in as many appearances, was utterly unthinkable. Needled by Zaheer, Border and his guards were in no mood to stick to the script.

McDermott had more motivation than most. Broad of shoulder and even more expansive of heart, the russet-haired young Queenslander had had a meteoric introduction to the international scene, taking 40 wickets in his first eight Tests after a call-up at 19, only to lose form and composure just as abruptly. Overlooked until the fourth Test of the 1986-87 Ashes series, these four weeks presented him with a golden chance to disabuse the sceptics. Some felt his style too aggressive to be pertinent in such a setting but his decisive late burst in the opening match had quashed that line of argument. Nothing, after all, stems runs quite as efficiently as wickets.

Imran was the only one of the three home quicks to curb Marsh, Boon, Veletta and Jones, who survived a close call for a run-out as Australia, having won the toss, reached 215 for three. By then Pakistan were in the wars: Javed stumped Boon while deputizing behind the stumps for Salim Yousuf, compelled to leave the field after a ball from Qadir had ricocheted into his mouth via Jones's pad; left-arm spinner Tauseef had damaged a thumb on his bowling hand. Border's run-out, though, left a gap to be exploited, and Imran steamed into it, bowling Veletta, Dyer and McDermott in a spell of 5-1-17-3. Bringing back Jaffer, whose previous five overs had gone for 39, proved rather less inspirational, Waugh spanking a six and two fours in the final over.

When Pakistan set off, Imran was summoned somewhat sooner than he would have wished. Ramiz Raja, Wasim's younger brother, had concocted a century against England and 70s off Sri Lanka and West Indies, but a breakdown in negotiations with opening partner Mansoor Akhtar over a single against McDermott saw Border throw him out for one. McDermott then bowled Akhtar, and when he held a dolly popped up by Malik off Waugh's first offering, the local demigod entered at 38 for three.

Imran and Javed rebuilt the innings brick-by-brick, soberly and stealthily. They had put on 112 in 25 overs when, with 118 more required off 15 overs, difficult but by no means impossible, Imran, of all people, mislaid his marbles. Border had brought himself on, his left-arm twirl flighted well but containing little obvious threat. With the equation tightening, Imran, having hit just four boundaries in his 58, sought to up a gear, essayed the wildest of wa-hoos and had his stumps scattered. The look of astonishment that swept over those finely-sculpted features was purely self-directed.

Javed, still relatively becalmed, was soon bowled by Reid and now it was McDermott's turn to flatten the barricades. Bowling the dangerous Akram, he mowed down Yousuf, Jaffer and Tauseef, all caught at the wicket, the tail docked with an over in hand. The final margin was 18 runs; it felt like 118. McDermott, the Man of the Match, finished with five for 44, due reward for maintaining a full length. 'You could have heard a pin drop,' recalled Boon. 'Only about three of their players, Abdul Qadir and a couple of young blokes, came out to the official presentation.' So long ahead on points, Imran had every cause to reach for the smelling salts.

Results

Group A						Group B					
	P	W	L	Pts	Runs/over		P	W	L	Pts	Runs/over
India	6	5	1	20	5.39	Pakistan	6	5	1	20	5.01
Australia	6	5	1	20	5.19	England	6	4	2	16	5.12
New Zealand	6	2	4	8	4.88	West Indies	6	3	3	12	5.16
Zimbabwe	6	0	6	0	3.76	Sri Lanka	6	0	6	0	4.04

Semi-finals

Lahore, 4 November: **Australia 267 for eight** (Boon 65, Imran 3-36); **Pakistan 249** (49 overs; Javed 70, Imran 58, McDermott 5-44). *Australia won by 18 runs.*

Bombay, 5 November: **England 254 for six** (Gooch 115, Gatting 56, Maninder 3-54); **India 219** (45.3 overs; Azharuddin 64, Hemmings 4-52). *England won by 35 runs.*

The Final: Australia v England
Calcutta, 8 November

Australia 253 for five (Boon 75, Veletta 45 not out); **England 246 for eight** (Athey 58, Lamb 45, Gatting 41). *Australia won by seven runs.*

One of the most endearing aspects of the World Cup, in stark contrast to its soccer progenitor, is the way it rubbishes notions of home advantage. Where seven of the 13 FIFA finals to date had featured the host nation, only one in three Prudential finals had done so. Given that Sri Lanka would wrest the trophy in Pakistan, that proportion now stands at two in six, with a solitary home triumph.

The much-touted 'dream final' had already been scuppered by Australia when England snuffed out the other co-host's flame. Rising from Calcutta's black hole with chins high and chests bursting, Gooch registered the first century in a World Cup semi-final as they avenged India's equally unimagined and unpopular victory at Old Trafford four years earlier. It says much for the organizers' quest for harmony that few, if any, comments were made about Gooch's South African connections, a source of no little consternation prior to the tournament. Gooch, who had played domestic cricket in the Republic since being banned from Test cricket for three years after leading the first 'rebel' tour, was cleared to participate; less than 12 months later, England's tour of India would be cancelled upon his appointment as captain: one slap in the face too many.

Indian magnanimity may have robbed Asia of its greatest day yet the alternative whetted only marginally fewer appetites: England and Australia, ancient foes reunited on a new(ish) stage. Border won a useful toss and opted to bat before an Eden Gardens crowd estimated at 70,000 (it would have been almost double that had the hometowners made it). Most rooted for the baggy and green of cap. They had, after all, had the decency to put out the accursed Pakistanis.

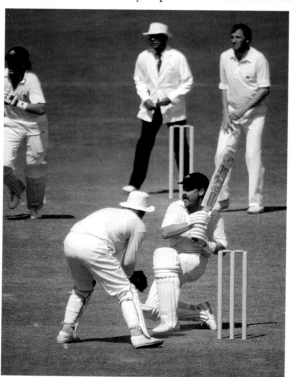

He is the walrus: David Boon sweeps John Emburey

Boon and Marsh scampered away at five an over against Phil DeFreitas and Gladstone Small before Neil Foster stalled them, darting one back to bowl Marsh at 75 amid an eight-over spell yielding just 16 runs. John Emburey's miserly off-breaks applied a brake of sorts but Jones pulled Hemmings for six, the walrus-like Boon served up some clunking on-drives and the 150 arrived in the 34th over, a decent launching pad. Now the Poms growled back. McDermott, promoted to maintain the momentum when Hemmings had Jones snapped up at short mid-on, slugged 14 off eight deliveries before swiping over one from Gooch; then Boon, the eventual Man of the Match, came unstuck, caught behind attempting to deposit Hemmings somewhere in the vicinity of the dark side of the moon. Thereafter it was all about Border's bustle and Veletta's vim, the rate pushed back over five an over as the last 10 were collared to the tune of 79: hardly melodious to Pommy ears.

England may or may not have been aware that the team batting second had yet to win a final, but if

Captain Cock-up: Mike Gatting moseys away as Allan Border is acclaimed for disposing of his rival captain, the key moment of the 1987 final

Waltzin' Mathildas: Border and co celebrate their conquest

they were there were few overt signs of distress, even when Tim Robinson went first ball, pads bruised by McDermott. Gooch and Bill Athey, a Yorkshireman transplanted to Bristol, added 65 in 17 overs, Athey and Gatting 69 in 13. Gatting took a particular fancy to off-spinner Tim May, lofting him over mid-off then swinging him over long-on for six via Waugh's illegal catch on the boundary line. So forcefully did the skipper bristle, he even reverse-swept him for three.

Cue Border's masterstroke: he brought himself on in place of May. Electing to overlook Imran's brashness in Lahore, Gatting neglected to have a look at Border before resuming the onslaught. As he sent down his first ball, Gatting turned around and reverse-swept: the ball flicked his right shoulder and looped up tamely for keeper Greg Dyer to complete the mugging. 'We were in real trouble until [then],' acknowledged Boon, describing it as 'the key moment'. Peter May, England's chairman of selectors, a robust opponent of the reverse sweep, had expressed his relief that the storms had left his television on the blink while Athey was making the selfsame cock-up against Pakistan: in the land where hurricanes hardly happened, electricity supplies had been cut. Now watching in person, he could only avert his gaze.

It wasn't over yet, not quite. Athey finally reached 50, off 92 balls, and Lamb lost no time in locating the fence as the first of the final 15 overs began with 102 needed. Now Waugh ran out Athey, and Border quickly sent down Paul Downton. Shrugging off a juddering blow to the lower abdomen – administered by Reid – with a typically defiant grin, Lamb kept swinging until Waugh bowled him as he pulled. DeFreitas wafted McDermott for six but that was the last moment the issue was in doubt.

'[That] was the major turning point,' coach Simpson would state in 1995 after his side had become the first to better West Indies in a Test series for 15 years. 'It was when the blokes realized they were good enough to take on anyone in the world. And the win against India in the first match was the thing we needed to kick us off. That was the big one. We got through tight situations. The enthusiasm was terrific. We also learned that unity, team spirit and camaraderie would take you through a hell of a lot.'

'Australia is back!' exclaimed David Frith, e0ditor of *Wisden Cricket Monthly*. 'And the cricket world's better for it.' Long ensconced in his native England after a protracted sojourn Down Under, Frith, admittedly, was quite open about having a foot in both camps. All the same, few Poms could place hand on heart and disagree with any vehemence. Not for a couple of years, anyway...

Multicoloured swap shop: Brian Lara (in maroon) and Moin Khan (in green) at the 1992 tournament, the first to feature coloured kit

Australia & New Zealand 1992

To paraphrase Lennon and McCartney, you had to admit it was getting better, getting better all the time. The fifth World Cup was the first to pit each participant against the other, enhancing matters on two fronts. For one thing, garnished as the field was by South Africa's post-Apartheid return to the fold, it facilitated a fairer and truer test of ability; for another, it allowed scope for a team to recover from a poor start, heightening the propensity for drama. Polluted as it was by quite the pottiest calculation yet devised to decide interrupted games, it was still the most enjoyable tournament to date.

Staged as it was primarily in Australia, home of Packer's Flying Circus, birthplace of flannelled tomfoolery as bona fide populist entertainment, it was also the most colourful World Cup yet. Dayglo flannels and matching pads, white balls and black sightscreens all made their debut. Ditto floodlights.

South Africa's late invitation was welcomed, although their squad excluded noteworthies such as that classy and prolific opener Jimmy Cook and that up-an'-at-'em all-rounder Clive Rice, both discarded on grounds of age. A generation, indeed, was in the process of vacating thrones. West Indies, already robbed of the retired Greenidge, omitted Richards; New Zealand had lost Hadlee for good; Imran, Kapil, Botham, Gooch, Border, Haynes and Marshall were gracing their last World Cup. Enter

Enterprise culture: Dipak Patel (right), who opened New Zealand's attack with his canny off-breaks, celebrates another wicket with Chris Cairns

Jonty Rhodes, fielder extraordinaire; Allan Donald, a white fast bowler fit to challenge Caribbean supremacy; Mushtaq Ahmed and Anil Kumble, Qadir's heirs in the vanguard of the leg-spin revival; Lara and Tendulkar, the new lords of the willow. Yet the lustiest bat belonged to dear old Kapil, whose rate of 125 runs per 100 balls left them all simpering in the distance. And the most restrictive bowler? Why, Dipak Patel, of Auckland by way of Worcestershire and Nairobi. Opening the New Zealand attack, an adroit if risky ruse hatched by his resourceful captain Martin Crowe, this reedy purveyor of off-breaks denied the early smiters the pace they craved, conceding an average of 3.10 runs per over. Ambrose, McDermott, Akram – you name 'em, he out-Scrooged 'em.

Winners of 37 of their preceding 44 limited-overs jousts, the Aussies were heavy favourites and massive disappointments. Jones was on the downslope, the support batting short of sparkle, penetration undiscernible: chirpy left-armer Mike Whitney was their greediest wicket-taker with nine – half Akram's table-heading 18. Although Border's corps finished the qualifiers with the third-best net run-rate (scoring-rate for minus scoring-rate against), fifth place left them bidding the earliest adieu yet by a host. An eight-wicket buffeting in Sydney from Botham and his fellow Poms left scars too deep to heal quickly.

Among the superpowers, West Indies, flying in the face of time-honoured typecasting, had the least impressive net run-rate. Now led by Richie Richardson, the Caribbean's erstwhile invincibles provoked even more profound dismay than the Australians. Their efforts in Christchurch, where they buckled to South Africa in almost acquiescent fashion, were a source of national dishonour.

It was the first time the teams had ever met on an official basis, a day brimming with wider significance and separate agendas. At first, all went well for Richardson and co: a cussed 56 from Peter Kirsten – one of the veterans the selectors did pick – held South Africa together but the target was still no

His beefiness mark two: Ian Botham

more than 201. Whereupon West Indies slid to 19 for four. Rhodes snared Lara with a criminally fine catch by his bootlaces yet the principal agent of humiliation was Meyrick Pringle, an unprepossessing medium-fast bowler with a shaggy hairstyle more becoming Iron Maiden's bassist. He it was who dispatched that first quartet, albeit with no little assistance: Richardson swung across a straight one, Carl Hooper guided a catch to slip and Keith Arthurton chased one that all but bisected the return crease. Driven by emotion, the innings never recovered. Back home, anger was rife and scapegoats sought. Administrators and players were held equally culpable.

Beneath Sydney's lights and fluorescent pantile roofs, came another historic match with broader implications. Kept apart in previous World Cups for primarily political reasons – though everything possible seemed to have been done to bring them together in the 1987 final – India and Pakistan laid on a much more gripping grudge match. Amid the crisis over Kashmir, the latest attempt to resume relations in the five-day arena had seen Pakistan cancel a tour of India in the wake of threats of disruption from Hindu fundamentalists. Happily, reported the Melbourne *Age*, 'the only politicisation' at the SCG stemmed from members of the International Sikh Youth Federation. 'Wearing the orange turbans of Khalistan, the homeland for which they are fighting the Indian government, they marched around the ground letting everyone know that they were barracking for Pakistan. Most people were too engrossed in the action to pay them any attention.'

Inevitably, there were some testy moments. Prabhakar's reaction to dismissing Malik, all have-at-thee-varmint, embodied the general mood; Javed and Kiran More, India's volatile stumper, traded insults in Urdu and received a stern wigging from the umpires. The game traced a similarly turbulent course. Tendulkar, the Man of the Match, played the only innings that was not frenetic, but Mushtaq, tossing up the ball with refreshing persistence, cut a swathe through India's middle order. Kapil counter-attacked, levering the total to 216 for seven, then promptly saw off Inzamam-ul-Haq, the youngster whose lumbering physique and dismissive air invoked the quintessential playground bully. Worse followed as Pakistan's so-called 'Big Three', Imran, Javed and Akram, all fell in the space of four overs; the last eight batsmen sank for 68 in a farrago of wantonness. Pakistan, possessed of more naked talent than any back-page rival, were every ounce as wasteful as their pre-tournament billing foresaw; India could only go downhill. And did.

Elsewhere, pride of place went to Sri Lanka, who pursued and cantered past Zimbabwe's 312 for four in New Plymouth with three wickets, four balls and, apparently, a gear or two in hand. Fuelled by captain Arjuna Ranatunga's 88 off 61 balls that daring day, they also beat South Africa, but heavy defeats by Australia, England and West Indies dulled their exuberance. In Albury, Zimbabwe, too, chalked up a major scalp, ending a run of seven reversals. Defending 134, Eddo Brandes, a prop forward of a fast bowler and a chicken farmer by trade, dislodged Gooch first ball, then, in the space of 20 balls, erased England's three southern Africans, Lamb, Robin Smith and his erstwhile schoolmate Graeme Hick. Houghton's doughties won by nine runs; then again, Gooch's charges, already safely through to the last four, were less focused than they might have been.

Pakistan's soggy collision with England in Adelaide, however, was much the most significant encounter of those first three weeks. The former, whose tilt with the Windies had resulted in demolition by 10 wickets, were all at sea against Botham and Pringle, king and one-time heir apparent, folding for 74 on a trying pitch. Pringle's magnificent reaction catch to see off Aamir Sohail was characteristic of England's sharpest performance in the field for many a yonk. In before lunch, they adjourned at 17 for one, whereafter rain held all the aces.

Under the 'best overs' system of calculation, whereby the most productive overs in the first innings were used as a means of revising the target, Botham and Smith resumed the quest shortly after 5 p.m. with 47 wanted off 10 overs – somewhat stiffer than the original 75 off 50! As it transpired, only two more overs were possible. Since Australia would wind up with a fractionally higher net run-rate, the point gleaned by Pakistan for a 'No Result' would ultimately define the difference between progress and an early flight.

Gooch contented himself with the observation that the rule was 'strange'. Besides, he added, the elements had made it all irrelevant, hadn't they? It is worth stressing that, according to the formula then in force in the counties, the stipulation would have been 24 in 16 overs – another manifestly unjust equation. Much as they warranted the brickbats flung their way, those who had tried to come up with a just and equitable solution – among them that *éminence gris* and font of all wisdom, Richie Benaud – deserved compassion.

Most Runs

Name	Runs Scored	Matches	Average
Javed Miandad (Pakistan)	1083	33	43.32
Viv Richards (West Indies)	1013	23	63.31
Graham Gooch (England)	897	21	44.85
Martin Crowe (New Zealand)	880	21	55.00
Desmond Haynes (West Indies)	854	25	37.13
Arjuna Ranatunga (Sri Lanka)	835	25	52.18
David Boon (Australia)	815	16	54.33
Sachin Tendulkar (India)	806	15	67.16
Aravinda de Silva (Sri Lanka)	724	20	45.25
Ramiz Raja (Pakistan)	700	16	53.84

The Great Match: Australia v India
Brisbane, 1 March

Hello Mr Lightning, how jolly nice to see you again. After the exhilarating slugfest between these sides in Madras five years earlier, who could have foreseen that the rematch would go the distance and then some? It featured starring roles for each side's premier toreador, all manner of extraterrestrial fielding, an all-but fatal foul-up from the best fielder on the pitch, and a final over (indeed, a final ball) to die for. And to think that we would have been denied such a spellbinding conclusion had the rules been even a teeny bit less ludicrous.

Australia, still seeking their first win after two defeats, opted to bat first, whereupon the redoubtable Kapil unhinged Marsh and Mark Taylor in his opening spell. Jones, though, was swiftly into his imperious stride. One mighty on-driven six off Javagal Srinath, an emerging new-ball operative, drew gasps as 'Deano' romped to 90 off 109 balls, before the wily Prabhakar induced a return hoick that threatened to puncture the ozone layer. Venkatapathy Raju's tweak retarded the middle of the innings but Steve Waugh (his younger twin was now part of the furniture, albeit not for this particular match) chipped in productively, as did the towering Tom Moody. The result – a passable 237 for nine. After 16.2 overs, Shastri and Azharuddin had taken India's reply to 45 for one when rain brought a 21-minute lull; when they returned their allotment had been cut by three overs (seven-minute overs, anyone?) – and the target trimmed by two runs.

The Jones boy: Dean Jones, not for the first time, was the fulcrum of Australia's batting

Prabhakar would say his piece after India stumbled out, citing captain Azharuddin ('too mild-mannered') as the root of most, if not all, evil. This, though, was Azhar *in excelsis*. Driving with a combination of delicacy and timing utterly foreign to any other batsman on parade, he pierced the boundary 10 times en route to 93 before a push to midwicket's right saw him run out by the left-handed Border's stupendous pick-up and unerring throw. Boon, deputizing behind the stumps for the injured Ian Healy, was enjoying himself no end, not least when whipping off the bails to send back the obstructive Sanjay Manjrekar. When Brian Aldridge signalled a bye against his account, Boon shot him a glare so withering – Kapil's pad had clearly been the culprit – the umpire instructed the scorers to convert it into a leg-bye.

And so to that final over, 13 runs and three wickets the respective requirements. Border had planned to use McDermott in such a situation but failed to take into account the reduction in overs and thus miscalculated, leaving the somewhat less daunting Moody with the monkey on his back. Kiran More whipped the first two balls, fullish tosses both, behind square for four; the third saw his middle pole loosened as he made room to glance – the blow shattered Channel 9's revolutionary

Grace and favour: Mohammad Azharuddin

'Stump Vision' camera. In trudged the injured Prabhakar, who pushed the next ball back, to Moody's left, and promptly set off in pursuit of a run that existed exclusively in his own imagination; in the event, Moody's throw was feeble, Prabhakar limped home, and only a sturdy bit of backing-up from Waugh forestalled overthrows. The heebie-jeebies were doing the rounds.

Srinath sloshed the next ball to Border, still manning midwicket, and sensibly held his ground. Prabhakar, however, had evidently decided he wanted the strike after all: stranded, it was all he could do to change direction before the non-striker's bails were displaced. One ball, four to get. Srinath drilled deep and wide but Waugh, at long-on, had only a few yards to cover and got under it in plenty of time, albeit only just inside the rope; to widespread dropping of jaws, it spilled from those invariably sticky fingers.

By now Srinath and Raju had completed one run and were turning for a second; aware that a third would tie the match, Raju scurried for the danger end as Waugh's throw winged in, defeating the lunging blade by the shortest of necks. Dick Francis would have been pleased as Punch to have tossed off a yarn like that.

Horse-sense: Martin Crowe, New Zealand's astute captain and master batsman, the 1992 Player of the Tournament

The Great Duel: Martin Crowe v Javed Miandad
Auckland, 21 March

It says a great deal for the adaptability of the modern batsman that the chap who took the greatest advantage of the fielding circle was Mark Greatbatch. This immense, whiskery fellow, after all, had made his name with one of the most stoical match-saving innings in modern Test history. On 14 occasions in this tournament his drives, hooks and pulls carried to the boundary: more than twice as many sixes as the next best. All the same, it was the runner-up, Crowe, who provided the horsepower – and horse-sense – that drove New Zealand into the last four.

Playing all their qualifiers on terra familiar, the co-hosts topped the table after the first week, outclassing Australia, Sri Lanka and South Africa by turn; nor did they let up. Not until the final outing of the preliminaries, against Pakistan in Christchurch, did they lose – and they had long since qualified by

Best Bowling Average *Qualification: 10 wickets*

Name	Balls	R	W	Avge	Best	5w	Econ
Gary Gilmour (Australia)	144	62	11	5.63	6-14	2	2.58
Mike Hendrick (England)	336	149	10	14.90	4-15	-	2.66
Chris Old (England)	543	243	16	15.18	4-8	-	2.68
Paul Strang (Zimbabwe)	253	192	12	16.00	5-21	1	4.55
Michael Holding (West Indies)	695	341	20	17.05	4-33	-	2.94
Bob Willis (England)	709	315	18	17.50	4-11	-	2.66
Bernard Julien (West Indies)	360	177	10	17.70	4-20	-	2.95
Damien Fleming (Australia)	272	221	12	18.41	5-36	1	4.87
Keith Boyce (West Indies)	312	185	10	18.50	4-50	-	3.55
Patrick Patterson (West Indies)	396	278	15	18.53	3-31	-	4.21

that juncture. Australia's resultant exit inspired a dust-up between two members of the printing staff at the *Sydney Morning Herald*, one Aussie, one Kiwi: the paper hit the streets nearly four hours late.

Wavy of hair and distant of demeanour, the almost casually fluent Crowe, already voted Player of the Tournament, had run up 365 runs off 420 balls at an average of 121.67. Only two bowlers had managed to dismiss him. Three unbeaten half-centuries had flowed in the slipstream of the unconquered full Monty that had kicked off the campaign in Auckland, where Australasia's other representatives had sustained a numbing hiding, supercharging the Kiwi pecker.

When Crowe returned to Auckland for the first semi-final, he did so acutely aware that Pakistan had improved immeasurably since their early shakes. His counterpart, Imran, back in charge after one of Javed's customary interludes, knew that eliminating Crowe was the key. He proposed to throw the kitchen sink at him then handcuff the mortals with spin: it never remotely looked like working. 'Bewitching, efficient and perfect,' rejoiced the Melbourne *Age*, saluting Crowe's mastery of touch, angle and placement.

He had reached 82 when, having added 107 for the fourth wicket with Ken Rutherford, his partner pulled at Akram once more only to sky a catch; as the batsmen crossed, Crowe felt his hamstring tighten. 'I thought it was a bit of a turning point,' he would state with typical understatement. Hobbling from crease to square leg and back, he made another nine runs before a mix-up saw Greatbatch, his runner, run out. It was to be his final contribution to a tournament he had done more than anyone to decorate and illuminate.

He had done enough, nevertheless, to lay the foundations of a decisive total, leaving the lower orders to capitalize as the last 20 overs produced 161. Pakistan were now confronted by the not inconsiderable target of 263, more than they had ever accomplished in a World Cup chase.

Patel soon ejected Aamir Sohail; Imran put on 54 with Ramiz, then 50 with Javed, before Chris Harris ended his careworn residence. Malik followed almost immediately. 'We realized that if we had wickets in hand at the end, even seven an over was quite gettable,' reasoned Imran, defending the deliberation that had seen him dwell 93 balls over his 44. 'But it just got a bit out of hand. We were beginning to think we wouldn't get close.'

Inzamam changed all that, thundering 60 off 37 balls with a supple grace belying that seemingly cumbersome frame. So disciplined for so long, the Kiwi seamers wilted. Nodding approvingly from the other end, encouraging and soothing as appropriate, was Javed. The scoreboard may have dissented – not

Cutting edge: Javed Miandad, the highest scorer in World Cup history, never knowingly beaten

to mention the match adjudicator – yet his was the more profound influence. The subtle improvisations were not quite what they were, yet he remained the quintessential combatant, summoning all his expertise in mind games to transform his colleagues from fretters to strutters. By gesture and sign; a word here, a wink there. Inzamam was run out with 36 still required, and Akram lasted eight deliveries, but Moin Khan, the 19-year-old wicket-keeper, helped complete the job with unnerving aplomb.

Javed was still entrenched when the winning runs came with an over to spare. Still smarting after being elbowed from the captaincy by a fellow from the privileged classes who picked and chose when and where he played for his country, here was cricket's answer to Roberto Duran, the most maligned cricketer since Douglas Jardine. Yet without that grit and spit, what price Imran's polish?

Farce show: South Africa's requirement in the Sydney semi-final underlined the inadequacy of the rules for rain-affected games; the target was in fact 21

Results

	P	W	L	NR	Pts	Net Run-Rate
Qualifying Table						
New Zealand	8	7	1	–	14	0.59
England	8	5	2	1	11	0.47
South Africa	8	5	3	–	10	0.13
Pakistan	8	4	3	1	9	0.16
Australia	8	4	4	–	8	0.20
West Indies	8	4	4	–	8	0.07
India	8	2	5	–	5	0.14
Sri Lanka	8	2	5	1	5	–0.68
Zimbabwe	8	1	7	–	2	–1.14

Semi-finals

Auckland, 21 March: **New Zealand 262 for seven** (Crowe 91, Rutherford 50); **Pakistan 264 for six** (49 overs; Inzamam 60, Javed 57 not out). *Pakistan won by six wickets.*

Sydney, 22 March: **England 252 for six** (45 overs; Hick 83); **South Africa 232 for six** (43 overs; Hudson 46, Rhodes 43). *England won by 19 runs (revised target).*

The Final: Pakistan v England
Melbourne, 25 March

Pakistan 249 for six (Imran 72, Javed 58, Pringle 3-22); **England 227** (49.2 overs; Fairbrother 62, Mushtaq 3-41). *Pakistan won by 22 runs.*

Eighty-seven thousand, one hundred and eighty-two persons (plus attendant media, officials and flunkies) witnessed it in the flesh – a new limited-overs record. A billion folk spanning five continents and 29 nations absorbed it from armchairs and barstools. After 38 games in 30 days the planet's appetite for technicolor spectacles, quite plainly, was far from sated.

England were fortunate to be there. In their semi-final against South Africa the rain rules scaled fresh peaks of absurdity when drizzle converted the latter's target from a manageable 22 off the last 13 balls to 22 off seven, and thence to 21 off one. 'That's the way the cookie crumbles,' Bill Lawry, commentating for Channel 9, proclaimed coldly; the crowd were vastly more sympathetic, booing as the farce ended. The losers' pursed lips and diplomatic comments did them nothing but credit.

When Imran won the toss, he admitted that his decision to bat was based partly on his concerns about submitting his team to a similar fate. The skies, mercifully, were clear, and remained so long into the evening. As in 1975, the depth of gratitude knew few bounds.

Fears that England had peaked too soon appeared groundless as Pringle, shot through with cortisone injections to ease a rib injury, immediately thrust Pakistan onto the back foot. Making up in intelligence and planning for what he lacked in spite, the lofty Essex all-rounder had the nervy Sohail caught low down by Alec Stewart, slowly making a name for himself as something other than the England manager's son, then pinned Ramiz leg-before mid-shuffle. Relief, indeed, for Hick, who should already have run out Ramiz: caught off a Chris Lewis bouncer but failing to discern the no-ball call amid the din, the opener looked to have made off for the pavilion when Hick shied from backward point – and missed. That said, the umpire would have been within his rights to have turned down any appeal, had he decided that Ramiz was not attempting a run.

Surviving bellicose lbw appeals from successive Pringle deliveries, Javed set about repairing the hull with Imran, mutual *bêtes noires* once again linking arms. Gooch had a chance to split them in the 21st over when Imran top-edged the habitually impressive DeFreitas only to spill a difficult catch on the run. Caution, understandably, overrode all, echoing their approach in the semi-final, during which they went 11 overs while mustering a paltry three runs off their own bats. In the circumstances, as David Frith emphasised in *Wisden Cricket Monthly*, it was indeed 'astoundingly brave'.

Only once the storm had passed did they begin to resemble their usual selves. Imran heaved Richard Illingworth's left-arm spin into the members' enclosure; Javed steered DeFreitas through the vacant slips to pass 1,000 runs in World Cups. When Javed pulled, DeFreitas misjudged and came in too far: the ball sailed mockingly over his head. The alliance had realized 139 in 31 overs before Javed, now beset by back pains and joined by a runner, reverse-swept Illingworth to point. Imran didn't tarry much longer, battering Botham to long-on. Only now could the frolics commence.

'He's the man, Inzamam!' chorused the Pakistani flag-wavers, and their man didn't let them down one iota, thumping 42 off 35 balls, the pick a late cut off Botham executed with staggering delicacy. By now England were looking laboured and harassed, the spark gone. The persevering Pringle bowled Inzamam with his slower one to cap an exemplary stint but the effervescent Akram smacked 33 off 18 balls, completing a rush that saw 153 runs pour from the final 20 overs. Another World Cup final; another stiff ask for the chasers.

Nobly as the puckish Neil Fairbrother sought to mend spirits, England were fighting a rearguard

Touch of glass: Imran Khan drinks in the applause at the MCG

action from the outset. All the more so when Aaqib Javed complemented his stifling and penetrative new-ball spell, dashing in from deep square to tumble and hold as Gooch swept Mushtaq, then taking an ecstatic half-lap of honour. The one batsman to dominate at length in the Sydney semi, Hick had made his excuses in the previous over, confounded by one of Mushtaq's countless googlies: at 69 for four the game seemed perilously close to up.

Though troubled by Mushtaq, Lamb, a controversial choice ahead of Smith, took every opportunity to assert himself, lapping the leggie for four with unsuspected subtlety. Dwarfed by that outsize bat and over-roomy helmet, Fairbrother continued to nudge and nurdle, eschewing booming drives (he only struck three fours) yet locating gaps with enviable precision, and darting between the wickets like a fox teasing hounds. Lamb launched Imran over cover as the stand gained momentum, whereupon Imran, teetering on the brink of manning the lifeboats, recalled Akram. His spearhead's fifth ball, a rapid inswinger from round the wicket, bowled Lamb, terminating a 14-over liaison worth 72; the next was a photocopy, wrecking Chris Lewis's castle via a limp glove. At 165 for six, with a further 85 required from 10 overs, the game had virtually outlived its appeal as a contest. When Fairbrother's plucky effort ceased with a top-edged pull off Aaqib, all hope went with him.

Not since 1979 had a final boasted as many as three plausible candidates for the Man of the Match award; now there were four, Akram justly pipping Imran, Javed and Mushtaq. Imran, 39 but looking a fair bit more venerable, lost no time in apprising the media of the wonders the spoils would do for the cancer hospital he proposed to build in memory of his mother: the fund to which his players, some more reluctantly than others, had agreed to donate a substantial portion of their winnings. He also took the opportunity to remind the assembled ranks that, by insisting on Qadir's selection a decade ago, it was he who had paved the way for a new path to limited-overs glory: attacking bowlers.

So why, pray, had Javed been missing during the England innings? Imran confirmed that that back ailment had indeed been the cause, then smirked: 'Didn't you notice how quiet it was?'

Guard of honour: Soldiers were a common sight duing the 1996 World Cup, much the most turbulent to date

India, Pakistan & Sri Lanka 1996

Bookended by terrorists in Colombo and a riot in Calcutta, the 36-match trek to the final of the first 12-sided World Cup was as turbulent as it was prolonged. The kindness of the weather spared us any of the decimal-crunching shenanigans that disfigured the previous two tournaments; in their place flowed other, more disturbing undercurrents. Political point-scoring, cultural intolerance, bad grace and Mammon proliferated. The opening ceremony was widely condemned as inept; announcer-actor Saeed Jaffrey introduced the South Africans as the United Arab Emirates, prompting the former to confer a new name on captain Hansie Cronje – Sultan. Yet all was forgiven, if not quite forgotten. In one of the most uplifting slices of poetic justice in the annals of twentieth-century sport, Sri Lanka gave the game a facelift and seduced the world.

What a far cry that eventuality was from the opening stages, dominated as they were by the repercussions of their exquisite island's unending civil strife. A fortnight before the first ball, the Tamil Tigers exploded a bomb in the centre of Colombo, persuading both Australia, the ante-post favourites, and West Indies – though not Kenya or Zimbabwe – to forfeit their scheduled matches there against Sri Lanka. They also reconvened their own rendezvous, the original tickets for which had sold out in two hours flat, even if the prices were equivalent to a local's monthly wage. 'It is Australia's blessing to be free of war,' observed Simon Barnes in *The Times*. 'As a result they have come to a dreadful error of vision. They think that cricket is actually important. More, they think that *cricketers* are important, that cricketers have no duties beyond sport and themselves.'

Others charged the Australians with erecting a smokescreen. Sri Lanka's trip Down Under that winter had swung between the acrimonious and the downright nasty: there were fears of retribution.

Most Economical Bowling Figures *overs-maidens-runs-wickets*

Mike Hendrick	8-4-5-1	England v Canada, Manchester 1979
Bishen Bedi	12-8-6-1	India v East Africa, Leeds 1975
Chris Old	10-5-8-4	England v Canada, Manchester 1979
Derek Pringle	8.2-5-8-3	England v Pakistan, Adelaide 1992
Bob Willis	9-4-9-1	England v Sri Lanka, Leeds 1983
Richard Hadlee	12-6-10-0	New Zealand v East Africa, Birmingham 1975
John Snow	12-6-11-4	England v East Africa, Birmingham 1975
Derek Underwood	10-5-11-0	England v East Africa, Birmingham 1975
Majid Khan	11-4-11-1	Pakistan v Canada, Leeds 1979
Bob Willis	10.3-3-11-4	England v Canada, Manchester 1979
Somachandra de Silva	12-5-11-2	Sri Lanka v New Zealand, Derby 1983
Meyrick Pringle	8-4-11-4	South Africa v West Indies, Christchurch 1992
Brian McMillan	8-1-11-3	South Africa v UAE, Rawalpindi 1996

Even when, the day after the opening ceremony, a 266lb bomb was discovered a mile from the capital's Premadasa Stadium, voices could still be heard alleging Australian paranoia. Cynics pointed withering fingers at the mutterings when a practice game was organized in Madras – Mark Taylor and his crew felt the city was too close to Colombo. 'It was ironic,' averred Peter Deeley in *The Cricketer*, 'that two nations traditionally at each other's throats – India and Pakistan – should join together in a display of solidarity to play an exhibition match against Sri Lanka before a grateful and enthusiastic crowd.'

'The reason we aren't going has nothing to do with cricket; it's a civil matter,' explained Australia's thoughtful and tactful captain. 'There's a genuine concern of life-threatening injury.' Pressed at the end of the tournament about whether he had any regrets, Taylor made a sincere plea for understanding. 'Put yourselves in our shoes,' he proposed, 'and look at the way we live in Australia.' Within a month, 35 of his fellow citizens would be gunned down by a crazed Tasmanian.

This was the World Cup's initial foray, not only into globalization but into the world of the big buck. Broadly speaking, it succeeded, even if there were those who shuddered at the unabashed conspicuousness of the organizers' goal. Emboldened by England and Australia's renunciation of their ICC veto – which brought democracy to the ruling body, and not before time – the subcontinentals tabled a bid to stage the tournament, offering the associate members $100,000 in exchange for their votes; the English 'bribe' amounted to $60,000, nowhere near enough to tilt the balance. The Pakistan-India-Sri Lanka organizing committee (Pilcom) got cracking. Corporate hospitality boxes, long a staple in Britain and the Antipodes, would make their first bow in India. Television rights, having fetched £700,000 in 1992, now soared to a whopping £20m. Throw in stadium advertising deals of £8m, Coca-Cola's £2.5m sponsorship and any number of puffs for credit cards and sundry other contemporary symbols of free-market capitalism, and it was small wonder Pilcom projected profits in excess of $100m.

Thankfully, the actors played their parts to the hilt. No fewer than six batsmen averaged 78 or more: Ranatunga, Aravinda de Silva, Tendulkar, Saeed Anwar, Mark Waugh and Gary Kirsten. Of the six leading scalpers, four – Kumble (15 wickets), Paul Strang, Shane Warne and Harper (all 12) – were spinners. In Warne, moreover, Australia had at their beck and call the man responsible for making leg-spin sexy. In the free-hitting, freewheeling Sanath Jayasuriya, Sri Lanka could call on the most electrifying batsman of this or any other World Cup.

No slacking: Sanath Jayasuriya's hurricane hitting made him the Most Valuable Player of the 1996 tournament

The main structural flaw was the reversion to two qualifying groups. Unavoidable because of the numbers involved – the ICC Trophy supplied three graduates – the downside was that it took 30 matches to scale the field down to four, and all too many of the fixtures were irrelevant or laughably one-sided. There was one cherishable exception in Pune, where, in the most memorable outburst of cock-snooking since the competition's inception, Kenya nobbled West Indies. 'It is like having won the World Cup,' declaimed captain Maurice Odumbe, who then talked his hero, Brian Lara, into having his photo taken with each and every member of the winning side.

While West Indies recovered their self-esteem, England left theirs in South Africa, scene of a depressing winter expedition that had culminated in a 6-1 tanning in the one-day series. What followed was easily their least distinguished World Cup to date. Failing to reach the last four for the first time, had they not been grouped with Holland and the UAE, Mike Atherton's lumberers would have been lucky to draw anything other than a blank in the win column. Nor did the captain's ill-tempered description of a local journalist as a 'buffoon' help matters. Had the selectors possessed the wit and courage to appoint the more creative and zestful Dermot Reeve, who knows? It probably wouldn't have made that much difference.

The most palpable missing ingredient? In a word, sparkle. While the world and his wife were scorching turf and peppering perimeters, England's four meetings with full ICC members yielded a less-than princely four half-centuries by four different specialists. No less injuriously, DeFreitas led the wicket-takers with a humble half-dozen. Spin, shamefully, barely figured. 'British Lion: weak in the paw, long in the tail,' scoffed one Indian reporter after the opening loss to New Zealand. 'England walked to the gallows like criminals rather than martyrs.'

In the first World Cup to accommodate quarter-finals, only one passed muster as a truly competitive entity. Abetted by Donald's unaccountable exclusion in favour of a second spinner, Lara fashioned a *haute couture* 111 against South Africa, whereupon Harper and Jimmy Adams, West Indies' own twirlers, shared seven wickets to thwart the new favourites. While Jayasuriya whizzed Sri Lanka past pedestrian England, there was rancour aplenty in the aftermath of Pakistan's tame defeat by India. One religious group sacrificed a camel to bring Pakistan luck, distributing the flesh among Karachi's disadvantaged; the prayers went unanswered. His ruptured side muscles may have saved him from participating but Akram, Pakistan's captain, was still burned in effigy. The ongoing bribes scandal had led many to detect a calculated withdrawal.

More deserving of preservation, and for all the right reasons, was the run-stocked affair in Madras, where Harris and Germon rallied New Zealand from 44 for three to a challenging 286, 14 more than the highest second innings of the tournament to date. Oozing derision, the Waughs converted a mountain into a molehill, Mark reeling off his third century to ensure that Group A furnished all four semi-finalists.

The Great Duel: Sachin Tendulkar v Shane Warne
Bombay, 27 February

The day before, the greater part of the city had ground to a standstill. A strike had been staged by Dalit, Muslim and left-leaning political groups in protest against the Shiv Sena government, for, among other things, dropping cases against party activists alleged to have committed atrocities against Dalits and Muslims. As 40,000 folk descended on the Wankhede Stadium for a day-night bash, a special distraction was expected, nay, demanded. They were not disappointed.

The focal point, naturally, was Tendulkar, the local lad made disgustingly good. In his previous match, in Gwalior, the curly-locked professor's son had not so much overshadowed as overwhelmed Lara, even if his only challenger for the title of world batting champion had been sawn off in distinctly dodgy fashion. 'He was more than confident,' asserted Mike Marqusee in his insightful diary, *War Minus The Shooting*. 'He was ambition – middle-class, Bombay ambition – personified. He wanted to show the world what he could do.' The crowd, for their part, wanted him to show them that Warne wasn't all he was cracked up to be, to put him in his place. Indians pride themselves, not merely in their capacity for bowling spin, but for repelling it. Imagine Muhammad Ali clambering into the same ring as Sugar Ray Leonard: here was cricket's dream debate. Sport as art.

This was Australia's second outing, their first against decent opposition. In the wake of the Colombo calamities, Warne and his teammates had friends to make and people to influence. Mark Waugh, Taylor's opening partner, proceeded to do his level best, following up a century against Kenya with another, even more disarming hundred, all pristine classicism and minimal perspiration. Bar his captain, all the same, the support was barely worthy of the name, the last seven wickets toppling for 26, four in the final over.

Toss-up: Shane Warne unleashes another languid leg-break, or was it a googly?

Set 259, India staggered out of the blocks, Damien Fleming removing Ajay Jadeja and Vinod Kambli before the score had scaled double figures. More experimental than Waugh, Tendulkar watched tolerantly from the other end then cut loose. Urged to compromise by those who believed him to be too adventurous, his consistency in Tests had yet to translate into the double- and triple-hundreds chalked up by Lara. In this context, though, adventure was, if not paramount, then certainly desirable.

Of the 63 runs he and the young prince purloined for the third wicket, Azharuddin, hardly a slouch,

Masterly: Sachin Tendulkar, the pride of India

stumped up 10. The audience bellowed approval – 'Sachin, Sachin' – then hushed at the entrance of Warne. 'I cannot recall a batsman since Barry Richards and Graeme Pollock who made my heart thump the way Tendulkar does, or, for that matter, a bowler so wonderful to watch as Warne,' raved Mark Nicholas in the *Daily Telegraph*, anticipating the duel with boyish breathlessness.

A less resolute man than Warne might have chucked in the towel after the opening round. Ambling in off four or five seemingly absent-minded paces, he tossed up his first teaser: Tendulkar tonked it straight back over his head – for six. The next was thwacked in the same direction, only lower; the ball burst through Warne's fingertips. A conventional leg-break was sliced over the slips for four: 10 off the over. Yet Warne, as befits a man blessed with supreme confidence, refused to be cowed.

Taylor did his bit, hemming Tendulkar with four close fielders. Warne fused flight, turn, length and line, confining ambition to singles. From his next half-dozen overs but a dozen runs were unearthed. When Sanjay Manjrekar failed to make contact with a leggie, he waved a hand, frustration and bemusement plain. The benefits, not for the first time, accrued to others. Obliged to turn his bullets on the supporting cast, Tendulkar had reached 90 off 84 balls when, spotting him prancing down the track, Mark Waugh served up a faster, flatter, more lateral off-break, so lateral it was called a wide: Healy whisked off the bails, wrapping up the Man of the Match award for the bowler. From then on, despite ultimately pulling up just 17 runs short, the chase was doomed.

In literal terms, Warne's sole victim was Nayan Mongia, deceived by a slower one. That, though, was a secondary consideration, as was his analysis of 10–1–28–1. He was the only bowler in the match to concede his runs at less than four an over, but that, too, paled into insignificance beside his main accomplishment. Australia's genius had disarmed his counterpart, halving his options, hastening his demise. If ever a scoreboard entry lied through its teeth, it was the one that read 'S R Tendulkar st Healy b M Waugh'.

Most Centuries

Name	Hundreds	Matches
Mark Waugh	3	12
Ramiz Raja	3	16
Viv Richards	3	23
Geoff Marsh	2	13
Glenn Turner	2	14
Gordon Greenidge	2	15
Sachin Tendulkar	2	15
David Boon	2	16
Aamir Sohail	2	16
Aravinda de Silva	2	20

World Cup Records 1975-96

World Cup
England 99

C'mon Aussie, c'mon: Damien Fleming bowls Courtney Walsh to settle the most dramatic of World Cup semi-finals

Michael Bevan drives during his 69

The Great Match: Australia v West Indies
Mohali, 14 March

It had a lot to live down to. In the first semi-final, Eden Gardens had been reborn as Hell Park. Relinquishing two wickets in the opening over but rallying through de Silva's icy composure, Sri Lanka were cruising home when, ire stoked by the sight of seven of their idols slinking away for 22 runs, disgruntled home supporters began venting. Bottles were cast on to the outfield; seats were burned.

As the mayhem spread, Clive Lloyd, the match referee, herded the protagonists off the field for a quarter of an hour, tried to resume but then awarded the game to Sri Lanka by default. Since the hosts still required another 132 from 95 balls with their ninth pair in harness, the dearth of protests was unsurprising. That said, the shamefaced home board did request, albeit forlornly, that Sri Lanka be declared winners on run-rate. Remorse was apparent even as the game was being abandoned. One banner said it all, 'Congratulation [sic] Sri Lanka, we are sorry'.

Variously characterized, post-Pune, as 'shabby', 'desultory' and 'disastrous', West Indies had done marvellously well to get this far after their caning by Kenya. Winning when it mattered, they had disposed of Australia in their first post-Pune assignment as Lara (60) outdid Warne (0–30). Now, in their opening salvoes, Ambrose inflicted ducks on Waugh Minor and Ricky Ponting (a centurian when the teams met in Jaipur) while Ian Bishop castled Taylor and Waugh Major. At 15 for four, a rout beckoned. Taylor's decision to bat first on a grassy pitch was not hailed for its prescience.

Stuart Law and Michael Bevan hauled Australia towards respectability, putting on 138 in 32 overs, mingling heads-down doggedness with mounting craftiness. Nevertheless, a requirement of 208 seemed most unlikely to extend the opposition. After 41 overs of control and command, indeed, they were in the luxurious position of 165 for two. Lara had rattled up a run-a-ball 45 during a 68-run alliance for the second wicket with Shivnarine Chanderpaul, an astute if ungainly left-hander. Still entrenched, Chanderpaul had subsequently been joined by his buoyant captain in an unbroken stand currently worth 72. Richardson, having announced his intention to retire after the tournament, was going out with a substantial bang.

The whimpering set in when Chanderpaul, stricken by cramp, holed out off the curmudgeonly pace of Glenn McGrath. Overeager, perhaps, to get the job done, Richardson elevated his hitters, Harper and Ottis Gibson, accentuating the pressure on those of more pragmatic virtue. Warne, who had dismissed opener Courtney Browne with his first ball, was now in his second spell. Buzzing targets like a Spitfire, he strafed Gibson, Adams and Bishop in the space of three overs. Twenty-nine were added while six lemmings hurtled over the precipice.

Fortunately, Richardson remained, and he duly drilled the first ball of the final over for four: six to get. For some reason best known to himself, he then called Ambrose for a needlessly risky single and saw his partner run out. Having surrendered the strike, he could only look back in anguish as Walsh, the last man, flailed at his initial offering from Fleming and heard the death-rattle. Never in a World Cup had defeat been plucked so effortlessly from the clutches of victory. If Warne was the rightful Man of the Match, neither was there any dispute about the Sap of the Match.

Results

Group A						Group B					
	P	**W**	**L**	**Pts**	**Net Run-Rate**		**P**	**W**	**L**	**Pts**	**Net Run-Rate**
Sri Lanka	5	5	0	★10	1.64	**South Africa**	5	5	0	10	2.06
Australia	5	3	2	6	0.88	**Pakistan**	5	4	1	8	0.99
India	5	3	2	6	0.47	**New Zealand**	5	3	2	6	0.54
West Indies	5	2	3	4	-0.12	**England**	5	2	3	4	0.07
Zimbabwe	5	1	4	2	-0.95	**UAE**	5	1	4	2	-1.83
Kenya	5	1	4	2	-1.03	**Holland**	5	0	5	0	-1.95

★ Includes two forfeits

Quarter-finals
Faisalabad, 9 March: **England 235 for eight** (DeFreitas 67); **Sri Lanka 236 for five** (40.4 overs; Jayasuriya 82). *Sri Lanka won by five wickets.*

Bangalore, 9 March: **India 287 for eight** (Sidhu 93); **Pakistan 248 for nine** (49 overs★; Sohail 55, Prasad 3-45). *India won by 39 runs.*

★ Docked one over for slow over-rate.

Karachi, 11 March: **West Indies 264 for eight** (Lara 111, Chanderpaul 56); **South Africa 245** (49.3 overs, Harper 4-47). *West Indies won by 19 runs.*

Madras, 11 March: **New Zealand 286 for nine** (Harris 130, Germon 89); **Australia 289 for four** (47.5 overs; M Waugh 110, S Waugh 59 not out). *Australia won by six wickets.*

Semi-finals
Calcutta, 13 March: **Sri Lanka 251 for eight** (de Silva 66, Mahanama 58, Srinath 3-34); **India 120 for eight** (34.1 overs; Tendulkar 65, Jayasuriya 3-12). *Sri Lanka awarded match after it was abandoned owing to crowd disturbances.*

Mohali, 14 March: **Australia 207 for eight** (Law 72, Bevan 69); **West Indies 202** (49.3 overs; Chanderpaul 80, Richardson 49 not out, Warne 4-36). *Australia won by five runs.*

Unsung hero: Asanka Gurusinha's resourceful knock in the final was all but forgotten amid the plaudits for Aravinda de Silva

The Final: Australia v Sri Lanka
Lahore, 17 March

Australia 241 for seven (Taylor 74, Ponting 45, de Silva 3-42); **Sri Lanka 245 for three** (46.2 overs; de Silva 107 not out, Gurusinha 65, Ranatunga 47 not out). *Sri Lanka won by seven wickets.*

'Out of a World Cup contaminated by suspicion and ill-will,' rejoiced Alan Lee in *The Times*, 'a result to make the spirit soar.' Even a few Australians might have been inclined to cheer those inarguable sentiments. Yet it wasn't merely the ends that stirred those of a neutral and/or romantic disposition. The means aroused even more goosebumps.

If ever a team had a motive for revenge, Sri Lanka did, much as Ranatunga was keen to play down such a factor. Already needled by their opponents' refusal to play in Colombo, de Silva and his fellow precious mettles were further piqued when the Australian team filed away from the pre-match ceremony without waiting for the Sri Lankan anthem. It seemed they had mistaken the Pakistani anthem for that of their opponents. Innocent, yes, but somehow indicative of an unbridgeable divide.

Pakistan's failure to qualify led to a reported $6m offer by the Bengal Cricket Association to relocate the final from intimate Gadaffi Stadium, capacity 28,500, to Eden Gardens, capacity 110,000; the Pakistan board resisted. More creditable yet was the invitation issued by Javed to Bal Thackeray, notorious leader of the extreme right-wing Shiv Sena party, to be his guest of honour. Thackeray had made it abundantly clear, on more than one occasion, that Javed and his colleagues were unwelcome in his homeland; Pakistan had twice called off tours after he had threatened to prove it. In 1992 his supporters dug up the pitch in Bombay 48 hours before they were due in town. 'Let him feel he will be the guest of all Pakistan,' said Javed. 'I hope Mr Thackeray accepts the invitation and proves that sport unites, and not divides.'

Previous Cup final captains were all present in various capacities — and largely correct. Resplendent

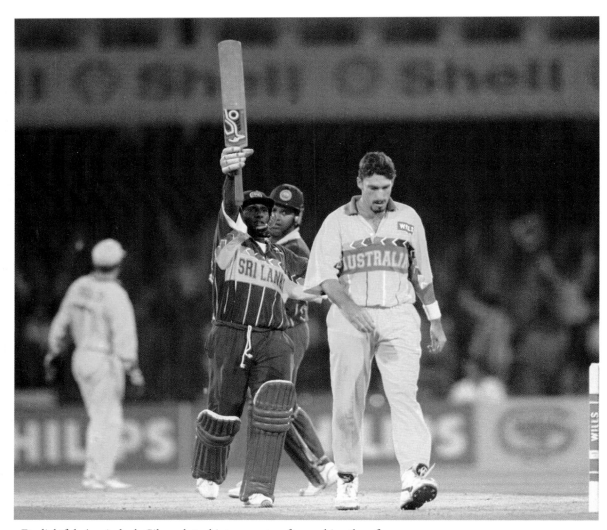

De-lightful: Aravinda de Silva salutes his teammates after reaching three figures

in white robes – as befits a would-be Prime Minister of a Muslim nation – Imran delivered his pitch report to the cameras and pronounced the surface 'full of runs'. While Ian Chappell played MC, Clive Lloyd hovered over Ranatunga at the toss, giving the distinct impression of aligning himself with the blokes in Everton blue and Norwich City yellow. Ranatunga inserted; Taylor insisted he would have batted anyway. Then again, he seldom does otherwise.

Before long he was wading into the seamers, shrugging off Waugh Minor's casual early flip to square leg and propelling his side to 137 for one in consort with the perky Ponting. The bowling was listless, the fielding ragged. Having already used three of his spinners, Ranatunga summoned the fourth, de Silva, whose off-breaks had gone for seven an over against England. Undeterred, the conscript induced a mis-sweep from Taylor in his first over; Jayasuriya pouched a tricky running catch. The complexion of the game was never the same again.

During the next eight overs Australia lost three further wickets, de Silva having a hand in each. Turning one extravagantly to bowl Ponting, he lobbed one down the leg side at Warne, promoted to pep up the rate: cognisant of the plan, Kaluwitherana executed the plot with breathtaking stealth. When Waugh Major went to dunk Dharmasena over midwicket it was de Silva who swallowed the leading edge, on the run. Both Waughs for 25 in toto? Ranatunga would have settled for double that.

Bevan imposed his matchless aptitude for squeezing the maximum from the closing overs, nimble footwork enabling him to repeatedly step away and drive 'inside-out' like some errant hacker unleashed on a municipal tee. As the innings adjourned, none the less, the Sri Lankans were wearing the grins.

Briefly, forgivably, the grins bred impertinence. Jayasuriya, already ennobled as the tournament's Most Valuable Player, was run out chancing a second before Kalu spliced a pull, both committing hara-kiri with unseemly haste as 12 for 0 off eight balls begat 23 for two off 32. Opening his account with a sumptuous straight drive, de Silva endured an uncertain overture, interspersing wary defence with the odd ravishing glance or clip. Warne, of course, would provide the litmus test, and did, albeit hardly in the manner expected. Eleven had been pilfered from his first five balls when a googly befuddled de Silva, catching the inside edge: not a straightforward chance but one that the world's finest wicket-keeper would expect to accept nine times out of ten. This was the tenth. Healy was mortified; Warne's fury was loud and extensive.

Masticating chewing-gum and glowering with similar ferocity, the bearded, bear-like Gurusinha biffed a Warne full-toss for four: 15 from the maestro's first seven offerings. Gripping the seam with all four fingers in an attempt to reduce the onus on his sore spinning digit, complete control was beyond him, not to mention that familiar rip. The major hurdle surmounted, tentativeness gave way to self-expression, the third-wicket pair raising the 100 stand in 19 overs. Four runs later Gurusinha pulled Bevan to deep midwicket where Law floored a sitter. 'That's the World Cup gone,' Tony Greig assured viewers. More or less.

When Gurusinha was bowled charging Reiffel the game entered another plane. Ranatunga broke his duck by gliding Reiffel for four past a gaping Healy; when Reiffel inserted a slip he simply glided wider, then wider still. 'Really cute,' enthused Greig's fellow commentator, Geoff Boycott, a crease-bound roundhead able to espy (and envy) the daring in others. Head religiously over the ball, de Silva caressed consecutive boundaries off Reiffel, defeating fielders by inches. Forty-one needed off the last eight overs: barely half that were required. Ranatunga was dropped driving Warne straight back and chin-high; the next ball was straight and chest-high: Ranatunga creamed it over the midwicket rope. A glance brought de Silva his century and an embrace from his captain, who dinked the winning runs to the third man boundary with appropriate élan and cheek.

'We were just outplayed,' conceded the ever-magnanimous Taylor. The knowledge that the organizers' profits bore no relation to their own financial rewards was hopelessly lost on the Sri Lankans. For Ranatunga, especially, it was a moment to savour. Raising the most ornate trophy ever glimpsed in a pavilion, he conveyed his heartfelt thanks to the Pakistani public for throwing their support behind his team. He then rendered a more pointed thank-you – 'to Azhar and Akram for coming to Colombo when we were in trouble'. Eyes a-twinkle as he defused loaded press questions about the relationship between the sides, he was adamant, nevertheless, that he and his countrymen were not 'brought up' to hold grudges.

The words that reverberated longest, though, were those contained in the pre-match advice tendered by coach Dav Whatmore, a canny, cuddly fellow who in a previous incarnation, irony of ironies, had batted for Australia. 'Do not,' he urged, 'be afraid of losing.'

Most Ducks

Name	Ducks	Matches
Keith Arthurton (West Indies)	4	13
Kris Srikkanth (India)	4	23
Chris Old (England)	3	9
David Houghton (Zimbabwe)	3	20
Ijaz Ahmed, sen. (Pakistan)	3	20
Arjuna Ranatunga (Sri Lanka)	3	25

Chapter 5

Under Starter's Orders

Note: all landmarks between 1975 and 1983 were achieved off 60 overs, those thereafter off 50.

Key: HS=highest score; LS=lowest score; 100s=centuries; BB=best bowling; 4w=four or more wickets in an innings.

ENGLAND

Best performance: Finalists 1979, 1987, 1992
Record: Played 40 Won 25 Lost 14 No Result 1
HS (team): 334 for four v India, Lord's 1975
LS: 93 v Australia, Leeds 1975
HS (individual): 137 Dennis Amiss v India, Lord's 1975
100s: 6
BB: 5-39 Vic Marks v Sri Lanka, Taunton 1983
4w: 11

U for Underachievers

Given that they staged the first three tournaments, given the plethora of county limited-overs fixtures – England is the only Test nation outside Sri Lanka where domestic one-dayers outnumber those of first-class dimensions – there really ought to have been at least one pot hoisted by now. As it is, inconsistency of form and uncertainty of approach have increasingly turned optimism to pessimism. Undecided whether to employ a hefty hitter as opener or pack the side with all-rounders, low on quality spin, reluctant to experiment, the potential nevertheless persists. Knowing that they are in a position to make as many waves as Alf Ramsey's Boys of '66 should serve as sufficient motivation.

Key batsman: Nick Knight **Key bowler:** Robert Croft **Prediction:** Winners.

Ace in the Hole
Graeme Hick

Compared with waiting for the real Hick to stand up, Godot's pals had it easy. Last summer, the mild-mannered Zimbabwean whose talents forced English cricket to revamp its registration rules became the second-youngest (and third-fastest) man in first-class annals to rack up a century of centuries. More consistent away from the pressures of his adopted home, he had, none the less, been ditched and recalled no fewer than seven times when flown in as a reinforcement for the 1998-99 Ashes tour. With bags packed and return flight booked, he was drafted in for the second Test in Perth, fell for a second-ball duck then atoned with one of the most violent innings glimpsed from an England batsman since the pomp of Botham. A one-day regular through it all – maturing off-breaks and nifty fielding are additional assets – the vibes point to a chap weighed down by expectation gradually mastering the art of having fun.

INDIA

Best performance: Winners 1983

Record: Played 36 Won 18 Lost 17 No Result 1

HS (team): 289 for six v Australia, Delhi 1987

LS: 158 v Australia, Nottingham 1983

HS (individual): 175 not out Kapil Dev v Zimbabwe, Tunbridge Wells 1983

100s: 5

BB: 5 for 43 Kapil Dev v Australia, Nottingham 1983

4w: 4

E for Enigmatic

Subtract that remarkable victory in the 1983 final and they've lost as many games as they've won. Overly reliant on Kapil in the past, they now look a shade too anxiously towards Tendulkar, again with ball as well as bat. If runs are rarely a problem, especially not on slow pitches, wickets frequently are, especially on those surfaces declining to offer assistance to spin. Much will depend on the fitness of Javagal Srinath, a shrewd, leggy spearhead who has already proved a real handful on English soil for Gloucestershire. Expect Azharuddin, the most-capped player in limited-overs history, to loom large in his fourth World Cup. May his brow never furrow.

Key batsman: Sachin Tendulkar **Key bowler:** Javagal Srinath **Prediction:** Early flight

Ace in the Hole
Saurav Ganguly

One might reasonably anticipate the strokes of this son of a Bengali tin millionaire to err towards the carefree. Not a bit of it. Composed and correct, judicious yet unlaboured, in 1996 he became only the third batsman to score a century at Lord's on his Test debut, then followed up with another three-figure effort in the next match. A staple in the five- and one-day sides ever since, he has developed into a highly productive opener in the latter department, scoring a match-winning century against his Sri Lankan hosts in last summer's Singer Trophy final. That solidity will be critical, as it was that day, in setting the table for Tendulkar. Those gentle seamers have their uses too.

KENYA

Best performance: 6th in Group A 1996

Record: Played 6 Won 1 Lost 4 No Result 1

HS (team): 254 for seven v Sri Lanka, Kandy 1996

LS: 134 v Zimbabwe, Patna 1996

HS (individual): 96 Steve Tikolo v Sri Lanka, Kandy 1996

100s: 0

BB: 3-15 Maurice Odumbe v West Indies, Pune 1996

4w: 0

E for Expect

As in the unexpected. How many teams, pray, would have even dreamt of defending 166 against a batting order containing Lara, Hooper and Chanderpaul? Since that first dip of the toe they've lost the ICC Trophy to Bangladesh on a last-gasp leg-bye, their second successive defeat in the final. Even more galling was the cock-up by captain Maurice Odumbe, or O'Dumbe as the Irish press so cruelly dubbed him. Believing two runs were required from the final ball, he allowed Hasib-ul-Hassan to scamper the winner. And yes, their colours were lowered by the same foes last year, but coach Alvin Kallicharran's newly professional charges could still give the Zimbabweans a fright.

Key batsman: Steve Tikolo **Key bowler:** Martin Suji **Prediction:** A second win.

Ace in the Hole
Steve Tikolo

Had he surfaced in Karachi or Kandy, Kalgoorlie or Kidderminster, he'd be a high-profile jewel as opposed to a concealed gem. Blazing a trail in the vital quarter-final group demolition of Canada with 93, it was his rousing unbeaten 147 off 152 balls against Bangladesh in that 1997 ICC final that formed the basis of a formidable 241 for seven, whereupon rain and poor arithmetic meddled. During the build-up to that tournament he won a domestic 50-over event off his own irreverent bat, cracking 159 in the quarter-final, 243 in the semis and 124 in the final without once surrendering his wicket. For a side lacking bowling depth, his all-round assets are crucial.

ZIMBABWE

Best performance: 5th Group A, 1996

Record: Played 26 Won 3 Lost 22 No Result 1

HS (team): 312 for four v Sri Lanka, New Plymouth 1992

LS: 134 v England, Albury 1992

HS (individual): 142 David Houghton v New Zealand, Hyderabad 1987

100s: 2

BB: 4-21 Eddo Brandes v England, Albury 1992

4w: 2

T for Tentative

Any side capable of scoring 134 and still prevailing, as it did against England in the 1992 tournament, has to have something in the blood worth bottling. By the same token, three wins in 26 World Cup outings tell their own deflating tale. Flower-powered and usually too peaceful for their own good, the most encouraging developments of late have been the strides taken by Henry Olonga, the first black to represent his country, and Neil Johnson, a hard-hitting all-rounder who has injected much-needed oomph with the bat since his arrival from South Africa. Terrific in the field, disciplined with the ball, they might just ruffle a few feathers.

Key batsman: Neil Johnson **Key bowler:** Paul Strang **Prediction:** Early flight.

Ace in the Hole
Murray Goodwin

Born in what was then Rhodesia, transplanted to Perth at 12, this dumpy 26-year-old was in the same Academy intake as McGrath and Ponting. While preparing for another season with Western Australia (having turned out for Holland in the interim), he decided to return to his native Harare, doubtless prompted in part by the retirement of David Houghton, so long the heart and soul of the Zimbabwe order. A hard-hitting stroke-player equally at home opening or at No. 3, he averaged 55 after his first six Tests, as adept against spin as pace. Known as 'Magic', as in Magic Gnome, an allusion to his comparative lack of inches. As the advert used to say, too good to hurry.

SOUTH AFRICA

Best performance: Semi-finals 1992
Record: Played 15 Won 10 Lost 5
HS (team): 328 for three v Holland, Rawalpindi 1996
LS: 195 v Sri Lanka, Wellington 1992
HS (individual): 188 not out Gary Kirsten v UAE, Rawalpindi 1996
100s: 2
BB: 4-11 Meyrick Pringle v West Indies, Christchurch 1992
4w: 1

T for Ticked

As in all the boxes. Hansie Cronje, a shrewd, hard-headed captain, can call on adaptable batsmen, liberty-defying seamers, the planet's most fearsome fast bowler and the most dazzling fielder in the cosmos. At the time of writing, that salty old dog of an off-spinner Pat Symcox was taking the new ball and they had just lifted the 'mini-World Cup' in Bangladesh, underscoring their status as favourites for the real McCoy. They also have that victory in last summer's Texaco series in England to warm them. A fully fit Lance Klusener, their most potent hitter, would be handy, similarly a reliable opening pair. Only the crowds, one suspects, can stop them.

Key batsman: Daryll Cullinan **Key bowler:** Allan Donald **Prediction:** Finalists.

Ace in the Hole
Jacques Kallis

The world's next great all-rounder? At 23, this sturdy lad from Cape Town has overcome hesitant beginnings to hint at an Eddie Barlow in the making. Technically sound and versatile – he has gone in everywhere from Nos. 1 to 6 – his batting is one of the few dependable features of an often brittle order; how many 21-year-olds, pray, have saved a Test match? Possessed of superb hands – one slip catch in England last summer took more than mere breath away – he is also a canny seamer, quicker than he looks and apt to make monkeys of those lulled into relaxation when Donald and Shaun Pollock are off. As fifth change in the 'mini World Cup' final, he sent back five West Indians in seven overs. A young lion finding his roar.

SRI LANKA

Best Perfomance: Winners 1996
Record: Played 31 Won 10 Lost 20 No Result 1
HS (team): 398 for five v Kenya, Kandy 1996
LS: 86 v West Indies, Manchester 1975
HS (individual): 145 Aravinda de Silva v Kenya, Kandy 1996
100s: 2
BB: 5–32 Asantha de Mel v New Zealand, Derby 1983
4w: 3

I for Infectious

Three years on and the victors are still counting the spoils. As recently as last autumn, each member of the 1996 side was gifted a block of land in Colombo. The impact of that cockle-warming display was incalculable. It invested the side with the confidence to go where no side had gone before, to wit that monumental 952 for six against India. Fired by possibility, there is now no more passionate cricketing hotbed than this tragically war-torn island. If the batting still resides in exuberant, experienced hands, the bowling may be too dependent on one man – Mr Muralitharan – to allow them to become the second country to retain the trophy. The health of Chaminda Vaas, the sole pace menace, remains of critical concern.
Key batsman: Aravinda de Silva **Key bowler:** Chaminda Vaas
Prediction: Semi-finalists.

Ace in the Hole
Muttiah Muralitharan

At a dinner given in his honour by his club, Tamil Union, marking this much-maligned spinner's historic 16-wicket bag at The Oval last August, the second fattest by a slow bowler in a Test, he dug into his own pocket and donated £1000 to the club's development project. Proof, indubitably, of a commendably broad perspective. Unable to straighten his arm – or so he claims and doctors concur – his action has been a constant source of soaring eyebrows; one unseemly outburst by David Lloyd, the England coach, almost cost the latter his job. That notwithstanding, he has restored vibrancy and invention to the off-break, reviving an art in danger of permanent hibernation. One of only two Tamils in the regular XI, a chap to be cherished as well as feared.

AUSTRALIA

Best performance: Winners 1987
Record: Played 37 Won 22 Lost 15
HS (team): 328 for five v Sri Lanka, Wellington 1992
LS: 129 v India, Chelmsford 1983
HS (individual): 130 Mark Waugh v Kenya, Vishakhapatnam 1996
100s: 10
BB: 6-14 Gary Gilmour v England, Leeds 1975
4w: 12

F for Fitful

When hearts are truly in it, as in 1987, they can be as bloody-minded as they are in the Test arena, yet a certain laxness can often be detected. Is it all a mite beneath them? While the absence of Taylor and Healy, no longer considered horses for this particular course, cannot help but be detrimental, a renewed fervour has been apparent in recent times, as befits a younger collective. This was notable against Pakistan last November when Ponting and Adam Gilchrist underpinned a successful pursuit of 315, establishing a new one-day record. In Michael Bevan, moreover, they boast the condensed game's most consistent and ingenious runmaker.

Key batsman: Michael Bevan **Key bowler:** Adam Dale **Prediction:** Semi-finalists.

Ace in the Hole
Adam Gilchrist

'Not shy to give the ball a good bash.' South Africa coach Bob Woolmer's line on this all-action wicket-keeper/batsman fails to do the New South Walian-turned-West Australian justice. Lean-limbed and classy, his strokes are a good deal more orthodox than rustic, prompting no less an authority than Greg Chappell to advocate him as 'the next superstar of Australian cricket'. The greatest compliment paid to him, mind, came courtesy of the national selectors, who happily dispensed with Healy, the heart of the team and world's best stumper by a mile or two, in order to accommodate his understudy at limited-overs level. Promoted in various learned quarters as a future captain.

BANGLADESH

First appearance

I for Intriguing

Slated as the next member of the Test brotherhood, the passion is unmistakable. For all the understandable objections to money being lavished on a sporting extravaganza when the less-than-well-heeled populace were short of food and still recovering from terrible floods, audiences for the 'mini World Cup' in Dhaka last autumn were chock-a-block, sometimes as high as 40,000. The ICC even had the good grace to cancel the official banquet and donate $100,000 to flood relief. Next up was a tour by a strong West Indies A team led by Ian Bishop yet beaten 2-1 in the one-day series. A major scalp here would be just the ticket.

Key batsman: Mohammad Rafique **Key bowler:** Enamul Haq Moni
Prediction: At least one victory.

Ace in the Hole
Akram Khan

Axed as national captain for the ICC Trophy just five weeks previously, the man from Chittagong returned to the ranks in style in the first meeting with West Indies A, fizzing to 61 off 62 balls to lead a successful chase for 233, victory arriving with nearly an over to spare. Aminul Islam Bulbul, his replacement at the helm, was ultimately fêted as the first man to lead Bangladesh to victory in a series against a Test-playing nation, picking up the Man of the Match award in the decisive game with 52 off 65 balls, a brace of wickets and a frugal spell, but the sort of fireworks required to take the next step are more likely to emanate from his predecessor's belligerent blade.

Most Runs in a World Cup

Year	Runs	Average
1996 **Sachin Tendulkar** (India)	523	87.16
1996 **Mark Waugh** (Australia)	484	80.66
1987 **Graham Gooch** (England)	471	58.87
1992 **Martin Crowe** (New Zealand)	456	114.00
1996 **Aravinda de Silva** (Sri Lanka)	448	89.60
1987 **David Boon** (Australia)	447	55.87
1992 **Javed Miandad** (Pakistan)	437	62.42
1987 **Geoff Marsh** (Australia)	428	61.14
1992 **Peter Kirsten** (South Africa)	410	68.33
1996 **Gary Kirsten** (South Africa)	391	78.20
1987 **Viv Richards** (West Indies)	391	65.16

World Cup Records 1975-96

PAKISTAN

Best Performance: Winners 1992

Record: Played 37 Won 21 Lost 15 No Result 1

HS (team): 338 for five v Sri Lanka, Swansea 1983

LS: 74 v England, Adelaide 1992

HS (individual): 119 not out Ramiz Raja v New Zealand, Christchurch 1992

100s: 9

BB: 5-44 Abdul Qadir v Sri Lanka, Leeds 1983

4w: 9

I for Infuriating

By rights they should have emerged triumphant in 1987 and 1996 as well, but temperaments were found wanting. On sheer ability they need fear no one: logically, a core of Saeed Anwar, Aamir Sohail, Inzamam-ul-Haq, Wasim Akram, Waqar Younis, Mushtaq Ahmed and Saqlain Mushtaq should be more than sufficient to mount an irresistible challenge. Logic, however, tends to exert precious little influence when it comes to assessing their prospects in major games. Especially when injury (particularly to Waqar, their quickest bowler), politics and all manner of distracting internal disorders continue to take their unfortunate toll.

Key batsman: Saeed Anwar **Key bowler:** Wasim Akram **Prediction:** Super Six and out.

Ace in the Hole
Shahid Afridi

Nobody is too sure how old he is – official sources cite him as 19 – but so what? He can still whet appetites at fifty paces. A strapping boy capable of GBH with the bat and deceit with the ball, he had already appeared in 66 one-day internationals when he made his Test bow against Australia last October, playing as an opener but starring as a leg-spinner with five wickets. While everyone is worrying about the big guns he could well pull off the odd ambush, as he did in sprinting to a century off 37 balls against Sri Lanka in Nairobi in 1997 to break Jayasuriya's world best, rubbing salt in the wound by taking 41 in two overs off the record-holder himself. Now that's what you call gall.

SCOTLAND

First appearance

L for Learners

Two Scots, Douglas Jardine and Mike Denness, may have led the Sassenachs, but the national XI has never been closer to taking on the auld enemy between stumps rather than posts. Not that a Super Six clash is likely. Worcestershire were seen off in last season's NatWest Trophy, Derbyshire, Durham and Yorkshire all run close in the B&H Cup. They also took the Costcutter Cup, albeit via a coin-toss and bowl-out. Here by virtue of a stunning defeat of Ireland in the ICC Trophy third-place play-off – so surprising, they had to un-book homeward flights to even participate – a good long sniff of the big top should suffice.

Key batsman: Bruce Patterson **Key bowler:** Stuart Kennedy **Prediction:** Pointless not purposeless.

Ace in the Hole
Craig Wright

Scotland have not stirred much loyalty of late. First it was the Warwickshire all-rounder Dougie Brown, aligning himself with the Sassenachs and proving himself a useful member of the England side that won the 1997-98 Champions Trophy in Sharjah. Then it was Gavin Hamilton, the richly promising Yorkshire seamer, throwing his lot in with that stuffy lot south of Hadrian's Wall. All of which leaves coach Jim Love's attack looking somewhat ripe for the pillaging. Wright, 25, a right-arm seamer from Paisley who turns out for West of Scotland, resolved the issue against Worcestershire last summer with a nap hand of victims, including Hick and Tom Moody – Lara beware.

Highest partnership for each wicket

1st	186	**Andrew Hudson & Gary Kirsten**, South Africa v Holland, Rawalpindi 1996	
2nd	176	**Dennis Amiss & Keith Fletcher**, England v India, Lord's 1975	
3rd	207	**Mark Waugh & Steve Waugh**, Australia v Kenya, Vishakhapatnam 1996	
4th	168	**Lee Germon & Chris Harris**, New Zealand v Australia, Madras 1996	
5th	*145	**Andy Flower & Andy Waller**, Zimbabwe v Sri Lanka, New Plymouth 1992	
6th	144	**Imran Khan & Shahid Mahboob**, Pakistan v Sri Lanka, Leeds 1983	
7th	*75	**Duncan Fletcher & Ian Butchart**, Zimbabwe v Australia, Nottingham 1983	
8th	117	**David Houghton & Ian Butchart**, Zimbabwe v New Zealand, Hyderabad 1987	
9th	*126	**Kapil Dev & Syed Kirmani**, India v Zimbabwe, Tunbridge Wells 1983	
10th	71	**Andy Roberts & Joel Garner**, West Indies v India, Manchester 1983	

World Cup Records 1975-96

World Cup England 99

WEST INDIES

Best performance: Winners 1975, 1979
Record: Played 37 Won 25 Lost 12
Highest (team): 360 for four v Sri Lanka, Karachi 1987
Lowest: 93 v Kenya, Pune 1996
Highest (individual): 181 Viv Richards v Sri Lanka, Karachi 1987
100s: 10
BB: 7-51 Winston Davis v Australia, Leeds 1983
4w: 9

C for Capricious

They can still tan the ruggedest hides – as Pakistan and India discovered in Dhaka – but the bad hair days are fast outnumbering the good 'uns. Nowt wrong with the batting that the odd spot of electro-shock therapy couldn't cure, it's the bowling that vexes. Can Courtney and Curtly – Mr Walsh and Mr Ambrose to you – roll back the years one last time and blast the opposition into submission? With the possible exception of Nixon McLean, their heirs induce few tremors; nor is there a spinner with any obvious capacity to bemuse, though if Rawl Lewis extends his recent strides and Carl Hooper stays focused, they could well go in with their most impressive slow attack at a World Cup. Capable of beating anyone but better at beating themselves.
Key batsman: Carl Hooper **Key bowler:** Courtney Walsh
Prediction: Super Six and out.

Ace in the Hole
Philo Wallace

A burly, buccaneering Bajan of the old school, Philo Alphonso Wallace – to permit him the grandeur of his full handle – has it in him to entertain crowds much as Jayasuriya did three years ago. Hailing, fittingly, from a place known as Around-the-town, he needs to be tethered at the earliest possible opportunity, preferring to deposit deliveries over rather than through the field in true 'pinch-hitter' fashion – even in Tests. Returning to the international fray after a limp introduction, he took something of a shine to England's new-ball operatives in Antigua, threatening Viv Richards's record for the speediest five-day century with 92 off 51 balls. Hard hats mandatory.

NEW ZEALAND
CRICKET

NEW ZEALAND

Best performance: Semi-finals 1975, 1979, 1992

Record: Played 35 Won 19 Lost 16

HS (team): 309 for five v East Africa, Birmingham 1975

Lowest: 158 v West Indies, The Oval 1975

HS (individual): 171 not out Glenn Turner v East Africa, Birmingham 1975

100s: 4

BB: 5-25 Richard Hadlee v Sri Lanka, Bristol 1983

4w: 1

O for Overachievers

As if to demonstrate to the world that they were no one-man operation, the 1992 tourney, the first of the post-Hadlee era, saw them at their inventive best; nor were they that far behind four years later. Ability is not in short supply. Chris Cairns remains a dangerous all-rounder, Simon Doull is one of the most improved seamers on the circuit and Nathan Astle an opener to be reckoned with, as his century against England amplified last time round. Once again, though, for all that youthful vigour, for all the fluency of captain Stephen Fleming and Craig McMillan, they lack a batting linchpin, a Turner or a Crowe, and are thus more likely to annoy than threaten.

Key batsman: Craig McMillan **Key bowler:** Chris Cairns **Prediction:** Early flight.

Ace in the Hole
Chris Harris

Like Cairns a scion of one of New Zealand's best-loved sporting clans, his father, PGZ, won nine Test caps with a smile seemingly branded across his jolly chops. Here, though, is more than your usual tale of chips and blocks. True, 'Lugs' cannot match Cairns for explosiveness, but he is every bit his equal as a one-day jack-of-all-trades, whether southpawing his way to that vain hundred against the Aussies in 1996 or sealing his country's place in the 1992 semi-finals with a mean spell of in-swing against the Windies. Don't be fooled by the action, an arm-whirling, wrong-foot number that would once have made him a prime candidate for Minister of Silly Walks.

Chapter 6

The Venues

Once the preserve of traditional Test grounds, the World Cup has expanded over its last few editions to take in a far greater range of venues. This is in part the consequence of expansion – the first two World Cups could comfortably be accommodated in England's six Test centres. The 27-match competitions of 1983 and 1987, much less the longer ones that have taken place since, could not be so concentrated.

But, paralleling the experience of the Rugby Union World Cup, which went to out-grounds from its 1987 start, there has been the realization that communities which do not normally see top-class cricket will respond to it. A group match between two relatively unglamorous sides which would occasion little excitement in London, Wellington or Bombay becomes a real event in Leicester, Napier or Pune.

The last England-based World Cup, in 1983, started this process with nine county grounds joining the six Test venues. Seven of the nine will host matches again. Two have gone missing: Tunbridge Wells, whose World Cup day will be long remembered for Kapil Dev's extraordinary, catalytic 175 against Zimbabwe; and Swansea, the first non-Test ground to host a one-day international in 1973, which staged that 1983 Pakistan-Sri Lanka runfest. Other grounds will surely also find that their day of international action is long remembered beyond the city boundaries, as Albury's in 1992 is recalled for Zimbabwe's defeat of England and Pune for Kenya's overthrowing of West Indies.

This competition will not be quite as far-flung as the 1996 World Cup, when 27 grounds in India, Sri Lanka and Pakistan were employed. But it will go to 21 grounds – the 18 first-class headquarters plus grounds in Ireland, Scotland and the Netherlands. It would be theoretically possible to visit 20 of the 21 during the competition's course (dedicated completists can do the lot if they make use of the warm-up games, adding magnificently feudal Arundel and pleasantly suburban Southgate for good measure). Anybody who does will be, to quote George Herbert Hirst, 'very tired'.

None of the grounds is as big as the giant stadiums of India, Pakistan and Australia, but they do offer an immense variety. One didn't exist at the time of the 1992 World Cup, while another almost certainly won't by the time of the 2003 event in South Africa. Surroundings may be urban, suburban or seaside – and if none are actually rural, some feel it. The view may include a range of hills, a giant Victorian orphanage, a fourteenth-century cathedral or the ultra-modern HQ of the British intelligence services. Each is redolent not only of its association with events in cricket history – places where Bradman drove and Verity spun – but in some cases with those of other sports. Two venues have staged FA Cup finals; another is next door to the site of the first rugby union international; another shares its site with one of our most famous rugby league venues; one is a former racecourse and one a ground which was once a dog track.

Huw Richards

Amsterdam

VRA Ground, Nieuwe Kalfjeslaan 21B, 1182AA Amstelveen, Netherlands
Tel: 00 31 20 641 8525/645 9816
Capacity: 3000
Match: South Africa v Kenya, 26 May

The Amstelveen ground, on the outskirts of Amsterdam, is also home to the Dutch Cricket board (the KNCB). The Dutch have a long cricket tradition, with several clubs dating back well into the nineteenth century, but until recently all games were played on matting wickets. The 1990s have seen grass wickets introduced at two grounds, Amstelveen and Het Schootsveld in Deventer, with VRA's first match on grass staged in 1996. The VRA played host to its first three-day game last year, when India A visited the Netherlands. The Indians had the better of a high-scoring draw, the highlight a century by Rohan Gavaskar, son of Sunil. The South Africans are already familiar with the ground after visiting during their tour of England last year, and opener Gary Kirsten may be especially keen to visit again after scoring 123 not out in a 50-over match against the national team, who qualified for the last World Cup but were eliminated in the quarter-final stages of the 1997 ICC Trophy.

The host Volharding RAP Amstels (VRA) club, founded in 1914, are the current Dutch champions after holding off VOC Rotterdam and HBS The Hague (both clubs more than a century old) in a tight finish to the 1998 Hoofdklasse. Players involved in the competition included the Australian Test spinner Colin Miller, professional for the Rood en Wit club.

Getting There

Rail: Amsterdam Central.
Buses: From Amsterdam Central, bus 170, 171 or 172. From Amstel station, bus 169. From South/World Trade Centre station, bus 63. From RAI station, bus 169. From Harlemmermeer bus station 147, 170, 171, 172. From all buses get off at Kalfjeslaan. Enter Nieuwe Kalfjeslaan opposite church, into Amsterdamse Bos (Forest). Over railway, straight on for 1500 metres and follow signs to VRA/ACC/Pinoke until just before parking area, then take left. Ground is 200 metres on the left.
Road: Follow Amstelveen signs on highway to Amstelveen Centre exit. Right at lights here into Keizer Karelweg, which becomes Amsterdamse Weg. After 2000 metres turn left opposite church into Nieuwe Kalfjeslaan, cross railway, straight on for 1500 metres following signs to VRA/ACC/Pinoke to parking area.

Bristol

Sun Alliance County Ground, Nevil Road, Bristol BS7 9EJ
Tel: 0117 924 5216
Capacity: 8000
Matches: West Indies v Pakistan, 16 May; Kenya v India, 23 May

The Ashley Down ground celebrates its centenary as a county ground this year having succeeded Clifton College as Gloucestershire's main centre in 1899. Visitors have a simple way of knowing if they are in the vicinity as surrounding streets are named after first-class and minor counties.

The ground's history reflects Gloucestershire's rather chequered fortunes this century. It was sold to chocolate makers Fry in 1915, repurchased in 1932 and then sold again to Phoenix Insurance (now incorporated in Sun Alliance) in 1976, enabling the development of multi-sports facilities including an indoor school, a driving range and squash courts. Like Lord's, Bristol has its Grace Gates – a plaque at the entrance to the ground commemorates the county's greatest cricketer. Looming overhead is a giant Victorian building now used as part of the University of the West of England: as Muller's orphanage it provided accommodation for up to 7000 children while Grace bestrode the cricket world.

Australian visits have left particularly strong memories – a tie in 1930 and the tourists' 774 for seven in 1948, on both occasions before record crowds of around 15,000. The wicket is often favourable to spinners, although Walter Hammond is reputed to have defied Tom Goddard, one of the county's greatest bowlers, in the nets using only the edge of his bat. West Indies will be the most eagerly awaited of the competition's four visitors, not only because the city has one of Britain's longest-established Caribbean populations, but as a chance to see Gloucestershire's long-serving, immensely popular fast bowler Courtney Walsh in national colours.

Getting There

Rail: Bristol Parkway or Bristol Temple Meads.
Buses: 72, 73, 74, 75, 76, 77 from city centre. From Parkway 72, 73. From Temple Meads 8 or 9 to bus station then any of 72-77.
Road: M32 junction 2, signs for Fishponds and Horfield. Take Muller Road exit (3rd if coming from M4). Left into Ralph Road opposite bus station, left at end into Ashley Down Road, immediate right into Kennington Avenue. Turn left at end of road to ground.

Canterbury

St Lawrence Ground, Old Dover
Road, Canterbury, Kent CT1 3NZ
Tel: 01227 456886
Capacity: 10,000
Match: England v Kenya, 18 May

'If I had to show a foreigner his first
cricket match,' wrote Geoffrey
Moorhouse, 'I should ideally like it to
be here, during Canterbury Week.'
One of the oldest county grounds,
dating back to 1847, the St Lawrence ground is famed for its annual festival – the last to take place at a
county headquarters – when marquees surround the playing area. The distinctive air and sense of history
are reinforced by two memorials – to nineteenth-century batsman Fuller Pilch and to Colin Blythe, the
great slow left-arm bowler killed in action in the First World War – as well as the famous lime tree which
sits within the playing area, offering batsmen what Americans would call a ground-rule four for striking it.
Only two – the West Indians Learie Constantine and Carl Hooper – have cleared it.

Kent's successes in the one-day game have ensured that the ground, the largest county HQ outside
the Test venues, has regularly been filled for big occasions – never more memorably than in 1993 when
Kent and Glamorgan, first and second in the Sunday League and with 21 consecutive wins between them,
met on the last weekend of the season. A crowd estimated at 12,000, some of whom stood all day, saw Viv
Richards play the decisive innings for Glamorgan in his last big match.

Getting There

Rail: Canterbury East.
Road: From M2 take A2, pass first Canterbury turn, then take turn off for
Bridge. Turn right, then fork right and follow signs for Canterbury (A290).
This becomes Old Dover Road, ground on left. From city centre take Old
Dover Road turn at roundabout by bus station.

Most Expensive Bowling Figures *overs-maidens-runs-wickets*

Martin Snedden	12-1-105-2	New Zealand v England, The Oval 1983
Asantha De Mel	10-0-97-1	Sri Lanka v West Indies, Karachi 1987
Martin Suji	9-0-85-1	Kenya v Sri Lanka, Kandy 1996
Karsan Ghavri	11-1-83-0	India v England, Lord's 1975
Derek Pringle	10-0-83-0	England v West Indies, Gujranwala 1987
Paul Allott	12-1-82-1	England v Sri Lanka, Taunton 1983
Maurice Odumbe	9-0-74-0	Kenya v Sri Lanka, Kandy 1996
Ashley Mallett	12-0-72-1	Australia v Sri Lanka, The Oval 1975
Asanka Gurusinha	10-0-72-2	Sri Lanka v Zimbabwe, New Plymouth 1992
Kevin Duers	10-0-72-0	Zimbabwe v Sri Lanka, New Plymouth 1992
Chris Harris	10-0-72-1	New Zealand v Pakistan, Auckland 1992
Richard Illingworth	10-1-72-1	England v Sri Lanka, Faisalabad 1996

Cardiff

Sophia Gardens, off Cathedral Road,
Cardiff CF1 9XR, Wales
Tel: 01222 343478
Capacity: 6000
Match: Australia v New Zealand, 20 May

One of the newest county grounds, created in the 1960s when Glamorgan were forced to leave the traditional city-centre Arms Park ground by the redevelopment of the National Rugby Stadium (currently being redeveloped yet again for the 1999 Rugby Union World Cup). Linked to the neighbouring Welsh National Sports Centre, Sophia Gardens staged its first match against the Indian tourists in 1967 and rapidly wrote its way into county history when Glamorgan clinched the county championship there in 1969 in a match against Worcestershire highlighted by a miraculous innings from Majid Khan.

The square-on pavilion, a pitch once prone to uneven bounce and the newness of it all have induced mixed feelings among followers – Glamorgan's long-serving captain and secretary Wilfred Wooller said it was 'a quite delightful rural setting, spacious and well-treed, but somehow it has never reproduced the cosy atmosphere at Cardiff Arms Park'. It also induces shudders among Somerset fans who remember their county, then still to win a trophy, going down by a single run in front of 11,000 spectators on the final Sunday of the 1976 John Player League season – the day after they had also lost the Gillette Cup final. Undaunted, and reckoning it a better commercial bet than Swansea's St Helen's ground, which is council-owned and shared with rugby union, Glamorgan have made Sophia Gardens their main centre – moving the club offices here from the Cardiff city centre in 1987 and purchasing a 125-year lease in 1995. The benefits of a major off-season redevelopment should be evident, even if it did necessitate the end of the popular 'Shed' stand.

Getting There
Rail: Cardiff Central.
Buses: 32, 62 from station. Also 21, 25, 33.
Road: On Cathedral Road (A4119) just north of junction with A4161. From M4, junction 29, A48 towards city centre. Turn off A48 onto A4161 towards city centre, follow signs over the Taff Bridge and filter right into Cathedral Road. Right turn to ground, on right after about 150 yards.

Chelmsford

The County Ground, New Writtle Street, Chelmsford, Essex CM2 0PG
Tel: 01245 252420
Capacity: 5200.
Matches: New Zealand v Bangladesh, 17 May; Zimbabwe v South Africa, 29 May

At once symbol and consequence of the golden age enjoyed by Essex cricket between 1979 and 1992 (perhaps uncoincidentally the time when the Essex-man style of politics also dominated Britain), the County Ground is one of the most modern, best-equipped non-Test venues in England. The ground was first used by Essex in 1925, but was initially second fiddle to the old county headquarters in Leyton – abandoned in 1933 – then one of the numerous venues employed in the peripatetic period symbolized by the county's famous mobile scoreboard.

Serious development here started in 1965, when Trevor Bailey secured an interest-free loan from the Warwickshire Supporters Club to fund the purchase of the ground for £15,000. The pavilion, a square-on construction, dates back to 1970 and the scoreboard to the early 1980s. Essex, without a trophy in their previous 84 first-class years, took 11, including six county championships, between 1979 and 1992. Perhaps Chelmsford's most spectacular year was 1983, which brought a championship, the dismissal of Surrey for 14 and its one previous World Cup match – the most significant of that year's group stage because India thrashed Australia to steal into the semi-finals.

Getting There
Rail: Chelmsford.
Road: In city centre, near junction of A138 with B1007 (New London Road). Access by car is from B1007, then turn into New Writtle Street. Ground is next door to Chelmsford City FC.

Chester–le–Street

The Riverside, Chester-le-Street, County Durham DH3 3QR
Tel: 0191 387 1717
Capacity: 6000
Matches: Pakistan v Scotland, 20 May; Australia v Bangladesh, 27 May

Newest first-class county they may be, but Durham are hard to match when it comes to offering magnificent medieval scenery while you watch. The Durham University ground, used on their admission to the county championship in 1992, offers spectacular vistas of the cathedral. Chester-le-Street, inaugurated in 1995, has an excellent view of the fourteenth-century Lumley Castle. There is nothing else medieval about this ground, constructed with the express intention of breaking into the Test ranks, a closed circle since the admission of Edgbaston and (temporarily) Bramall Lane in 1902.

Only half a mile from the Ropery Lane ground used by Durham in earlier seasons, the Riverside has housed the club offices from the club's entrance to the championship. The hundred-acre site will eventually incorporate facilities for athletics, tennis, hockey, rugby, football, rowing and American Football plus a nature reserve and a housing development. The plan is to build a 20,000-capacity stadium in five modules in a horseshoe-pattern around the playing area. Two have been completed so far, with others to follow when finances permit.

Getting There
Rail: Chester-le-Street.
Buses: 734, 775, 778.
Road: From A1(M) junction 63, take A167 (Shields Road) south from roundabout. Stay on A167 at next roundabout, A167 becomes Park Road North then Park Road Central. Left at roundabout into Ropery Lane, then right into the Riverside complex.

Derby

The County Cricket Ground,
Nottingham Road, Derby DE21 6DA
Tel: 01332 383211
Capacity: 5000
Match: New Zealand v Pakistan, 28 May

Only The Oval can match Derby's extraordinarily varied sporting history. Initially, and until 1939, the ground was a racecourse – the grandstand with its copper viewing-dome is one survivor of this era and until the pavilion was constructed in the early 1980s players changed in the old jockeys' quarters. It was also an important football ground, staging the 1886 FA Cup final replay in which Blackburn Rovers became the second (and so far last) team to take the trophy three times running, beating West Bromwich Albion 2-0.

This history left idiosyncracies which haven't found universal favour – the pitch formerly ranged from east to west, creating the possibility of good light stopping play as batsmen were dazzled on sunny days, while its bleakness on less attractive days led one *Guardian* writer to describe it as not entirely unconvincing as an opening set for *Macbeth*. New Zealand may not be entirely delighted to return – on their last World Cup visit in 1983 they were destroyed by quick bowler Asantha de Mel en route to defeat by Sri Lanka. But they will find a ground whose amenities have improved considerably since. Derbyshire, who contemplated leaving in the early 1970s, instead in 1982 took out a 125-year lease and have constructed a pavilion, scoreboard and new stands.

Getting There

Rail: Derby.
Bus: 212.
Road: By Pentagon roundabout on A61 (Sir Frank Whittle Road) and A52. Well signposted from Derby ring road.

Dublin

Clontarf Cricket Club, Castle Avenue, Clontarf,
Dublin 3, Republic of Ireland
Tel: 00 3531 336214
Capacity: 4000
Match: West Indies v Bangladesh, 21 May

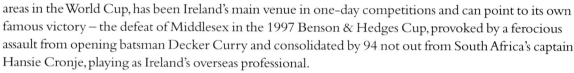

An inspired piece of match-making dispatches
the West Indians to Ireland. Whether inspired by
Lenny Henry's enthusiastic characterization of
the Irish as white Jamaicans or the 30th
anniversary of the most famous day in Irish
cricket, when a bemused West Indian team,
Sobers, Lloyd et al, were shot out for 25 at Sion
Mills near Derry, is unclear.

Castle Avenue, whose 122m x 118m
dimensions make it one of the smaller playing
areas in the World Cup, has been Ireland's main venue in one-day competitions and can point to its own
famous victory – the defeat of Middlesex in the 1997 Benson & Hedges Cup, provoked by a ferocious
assault from opening batsman Decker Curry and consolidated by 94 not out from South Africa's captain
Hansie Cronje, playing as Ireland's overseas professional.

The premises are shared with Clontarf Rugby Club, a First Division team who are the sole
exception to the rule that senior rugby in Dublin is played only south of the Liffey, and that the north is
left to the gaelic codes. Those with a taste for cricketing quirks and oddities should take a few minutes
while in the city centre to visit Trinity College. Here one can find a cricket ground which not only
occupies several acres in the centre of the capital of the Republic for a sport identified with the anglicised
ascendancy, but was also the home ground for the only Nobel Prize winner to have played first-class
cricket, playwright Samuel Beckett.

Getting There

Rail: Killester (DART).
Buses: 32, 44A, 54.
Road: Off Castle Avenue close
to the junction with Kincora
Grove, east of the city centre.
From the city centre follow
signs to Howth and Clontarf.
When road reaches Fairview
Park (to right of road) and
splits, continue down right
fork along coast road (Clontarf
Road). Castle Avenue is on left
after about 600 metres.

Edgbaston

County Ground, Edgbaston Road, Birmingham B5 7QU
Tel: 0121 446 4422
Capacity: 20,000
Matches: England v India, 29 May; Super Six match, 10 June; Second semi-final, 17 June

Lord's is really its only superior, concluded William Powell in the 1992 *Wisden Guide To Cricket Grounds* and Edgbaston's status is recognized by the award of its first World Cup semi-final. Warwickshire's home since 1884, it has been transformed since the Fifties through income from the highly successful pools scheme run by the club's supporters association – which became wealthy enough to make interest-free loans to some other clubs – and one of the largest county memberships. England's luckiest Test ground – a reputation reinforced by the ambush of the Australians on the first day of the 1997 Ashes series – it has seen record low scores by both Australia (36 in the ground's maiden Test in 1902) and South Africa (30 in 1924). It has also hosted three remarkable changes in fortune: Hampshire's victory after being bowled out for 15 in 1921, Sonny Ramadhin's calvary when Tests were restored to the ground in 1957, bowling 98 overs to Peter May and Colin Cowdrey's pads in the second innings after taking seven for 49 in the first, and, most significantly in a World Cup context, that last-wicket stand by Deryck Murray and Andy Roberts which took West Indies to that improbable victory over Pakistan in 1975.

Drinkers will find knowledge of fielding positions essential – bars are named after their notional locations in the field.

Getting There

Rail: Birmingham New Street.
Buses: 45 and 47 from city centre.
Road: From city centre take A441 south, turn left into Edgbaston Road (B4217), ground on right. The ground is well signposted from the M6. Use the ring road to link up with the A441 from other directions.

Edinburgh

Grange Cricket Club, Raeburn Place, Stockbridge, Edinburgh EH4 1HQ, Scotland
Tel: 0131 332 2148
Capacity: 6,000
Matches: Scotland v Bangladesh, 24 May; Scotland v New Zealand, 31 May

Older than many of the county clubs hosting this competition, Grange have been in existence since 1832 and have played at Raeburn Place since 1872. The site is packed with sporting history – the neighbouring Edinburgh Academicals ground hosted the first rugby international, between Scotland and England in 1871, and was Scotland's home ground until 1899. A few streets away is the famous Powderhall Stadium. The pavilion, which dates back to 1895, is a listed building recently restored with the aid of a large National Lottery grant.

Grange acted as Scotland's equivalent of MCC, running the game north of the border, between the dissolution of the first Scottish Cricket Union in 1880 and the creation of the current SCU in 1901. Unsurprisingly Scotland have used Raeburn Place for many years, in rotation with other grounds including Forfar, Broughty Ferry and the Glasgow duo of Titwood and West of Scotland (site of the first football international). The 1909 Australians were forced to hang on desperately for a draw, their 1921 successors were hit for 147 not out by John Kerr and in 1948 Bradman played his penultimate British innings at Raeburn Place.

As befits the home of Scotland's dominant club side, six times National Cup winners in the 1990s and supplier of national captain George Salmond and team regulars Steve Crawley and Peter Steindl, Raeburn Place is now the main venue for major matches, hosting visits by Australia, West Indies and Pakistan plus NatWest Trophy games including last year's defeat of Worcestershire.

Getting There

Rail: Edinburgh Waverley.
Road: From city centre, take Princes Street (A8), turn into Frederick Street, turn left after 600m into South East Circus Place, cross Circus Place, keep going straight ahead for about 300m. When road splits at end of Deanhaugh Street, Raeburn Place is the middle option. Ground on the right.

Headingley

Headingley Cricket Ground, St Michael's Lane, Leeds LS6 3BU
Tel: 0113 278 7394
Capacity: 16,000
Matches: Australia v Pakistan, 23 May; Super Six match, 6 June; Super Six match, 13 June

Often criticized for the eccentricity of its pitches and the behaviour of its crowds, Headingley, which celebrates its centenary as a Test venue in 1999, consistently produces greater drama than any other British ground, the desperately tight conclusion to the England v South Africa series last August being merely the latest in the sequence. Sharing a site with Leeds Rugby League Club, whose stadium backs on to the main stand, Headingley has recently seen off a threat by Yorkshire to move to a purpose-built headquarters at Wakefield and its future appears secured.

Noisily characterful, with its surrounding walkway and giant Western Terrace, Headingley saw a trio of extraordinary innings by Bradman – consecutive triple centuries in 1930 and 1934 followed by 173 not out in Australia's astonishing 1948 run chase – in addition to Boycott's 100th century in the 1977 Ashes Test and Botham's improbable heroics in 1981. Since Australia were shot out for 23 by Yorkshire in 1902 it has, none the less, been predominantly a bowler's ground. Hedley Verity's 10 for 10 against Notts in 1932 remains the best first-class analysis anywhere while nine previous World Cup matches produced the competition's best analysis (Davis), its most economical figures (Bedi) and arguably its most decisive spell (Gilmour).

Getting There

Rail: Headingley.
Buses: 1, 28, 56, 57, 63, 93, 96.
Road: M1 junction 47, then M621 junction 2, A643 towards city centre. Join A58M and follow signs for A660 (Otley, Skipton). Join A660 which becomes Headingley Lane. Left into North Lane, ground on left. From the west M62 junction 27, then M621 to junction 2, then as above.

Most Wickets

Name	Wickets	Average
Imran Khan (Pakistan)	34	19.26
Ian Botham (England)	30	25.40
Phil DeFreitas (England)	29	25.58
Wasim Akram (Pakistan)	28	27.42
Kapil Dev (India)	28	31.85
Craig McDermott (Australia)	27	22.18
Mushtaq Ahmed (Pakistan)	26	21.11
Andy Roberts (West Indies)	26	21.23
Abdul Qadir (Pakistan)	24	21.08
Manoj Prabhakar (India)	24	26.66
Steve Waugh (Australia)	24	30.08

Hove

County Ground, Eaton Road, Hove,
East Sussex, BN3 3AN
Tel: 01273 827100
Capacity: 5,000
Match: India v South Africa,
15 May

Hove saw some of the best of the early days of limited-overs cricket as the Sussex team of Parks, Dexter and Thomson took the first two Gillette Cups in 1963 and 1964. The ground mixes the old with the ultra-modern – the turf was brought here from the old Royal Brunswick ground when Sussex moved in 1872, the pavilion is essentially the same structure that saw possibly the most spectacular outbreak of batting pyrotechnics ever, 'Alletson's innings' of 1910, immortalised in John Arlott's essay of that name, in which the Notts all-rounder hammered 142 runs in 40 minutes after lunch and hit one ball so violently that it stuck in the wood of the grandstand. It is the only county ground with permanent floodlights.

The ground offers an excellent behind-the-bowler's-arm view from seats on the roof of the indoor school at the sea end, unfortunately not in use during the tournament, and reportedly an even better one from the blocks of flats just outside. Playwright Alan Melville noted both these and the county's tradition of exotic, high-class imports when he wrote, 'Where else could you lean on your balcony and watch characters with good old Chestertonian Sussex names like Imran Khan and Garth le Roux at the top of their form without paying a penny piece.' Like other seaside grounds it is prone to climatic conditions which scientists say do not affect the behaviour of the ball: players disagree; swing bowlers tend to relish both tides and sea-mist.

Getting There

Rail: Hove. Brighton is less than a mile away.
Bus: 7 from Hove Station, 6 from Brighton Station.
Road: From A23 into Brighton follow signs for A27 Hove/Worthing. Keep left, following Hove signs. At roundabout take second exit to Brighton (Dyke Road). Right into Woodland Drive then left into Shirley Drive. Left into Eaton Avenue, ground on left.

Leicester

County Ground, Grace Road, Leicester LE2 8AD
Tel: 0116 283 2128/1880
Capacity: 4,500
Matches: India v Zimbabwe, 19 May; West Indies v Scotland, 27 May

Occasionally described as uncharismatic, Grace Road plays host to a team sometimes seen in the same terms. Leicestershire, nevertheless, have proved themselves the outstanding county of the late 1990s with two championships in three years. Both ground and club were transformed during the reign as secretary and chief executive of Mike Turner from 1960. Before then Leicestershire had oscillated between here and Aylestone Road, moving three times before settling permanently at Grace Road, then owned by and shared with the local education authority, in 1962. Aylestone Road has its permanent memorial in the distinctive barrel-roofed stand known as The Meet, transported by the county on their last move.

The county finally purchased the ground in 1966, subsequently developing it into the small, but well-equipped venue of today. India and Zimbabwe also met here in the 1983 World Cup, when India won by five wickets and Kirmani took five catches, still a Cup record. West Indies, who can expect a particularly rapturous reception if they include Leicestershire hero Phil Simmons, will be delighted if they can recapture the batting form which brought their predecessors of 1950 the not inconsiderable total of 682 for two.

Getting There

Rail: Leicester.
Buses: 26, 37, 37a, 38, 38a, 47, 48, 48a, 68, 73, 76.
Road: From M1 junction 21, take A563 towards city centre, left onto A426 then right after one mile into Grace Road. From city centre, take A426 from inner ring road, Grace Road is a left turn.

Lord's

Lord's Cricket Ground, Wellington Road, London NW8 8QN
Tel: 0171 289 1611
Capacity: 30,000
Matches: England v Sri Lanka, 14 May; Super Six match, 9 June; Final, 20 June

The most famous cricket ground in the world, yet two-thirds transformed since staging the first three finals – only the Pavilion End, with its massive four-square redbrick Victorian Pavilion, remains unchanged among the major features. Remodelling for this competition include the new Grand Stand and the eye-catching media centre which now dominates the Nursery End.

W.G. Grace's unique contribution to the game and this ground – many of his greatest performances were for MCC or the Gentlemen – is commemorated in the Grace Gates, erected in 1923 with their perfectly simple legend 'The Great Cricketer', while the fact that the architect of the Pavilion was Thomas Verity makes it appropriate that his namesake Hedley produced possibly the ground's most memorable bowling by an Englishman, demolishing Australia twice in a day in 1934, though England have not won an Ashes Test there since. Host to 97 Tests, more than any other ground.

Getting There
London Underground: St John's Wood.
Buses: 13, 82, 113, 139, 189, 274.
Road: On the A41, on right going south just before junction with St John's Wood Road (A5205). From central London take inner ring road A501, turn north into A41 at Gloucester Place. From M1 turn left on to North Circular (A406) then follow signs to A41.

Most Wickets in a World Cup

		Wickets	Matches	Average
1992	**Wasim Akram** (Pakistan)	18	10	18.77
1987	**Craig McDermott** (Australia)	18	8	18.94
1983	**Roger Binny** (India)	18	8	18.66
1983	**Madan Lal** (India)	17	8	16.76
1987	**Imran Khan** (Pakistan)	17	7	13.05
1983	**Asantha de Mel** (Sri Lanka)	17	6	15.58
1992	**Ian Botham** (England)	16	10	19.12
1992	**Chris Harris** (New Zealand)	16	9	21.37
1992	**Mushtaq Ahmed** (Pakistan)	16	9	19.43
1996	**Anil Kumble** (India)	15	7	18.73

World Cup Records 1975-96

World Cup England 99

Northampton

County Cricket Ground, Wantage Road, Northampton NN1 4TJ
Tel: 01604 514455
Capacity: 7,000
Matches: Sri Lanka v South Africa, 19 May; Pakistan v Bangladesh, 31 May

Frank Tyson, who terrified batsmen here in the Fifties, said Wantage Road was 'a rather barren heath'; Aylwin Sampson felt it 'doubtful if even the most partisan supporter of Northamptonshire would assert that [it] was beautiful… a workaday ground with a no-nonsense setting'. This is another ground with a multi-sports history, the only county headquarters to have staged First Division football this century, the venue where George Best once scored six goals in an FA Cup tie for Manchester United. Northampton Town moved out in 1996 after almost a century of ground-sharing, allowing the county club to develop it as a cricket-only venue. Improvements started before the footballers relocated, with a new players' pavilion built in 1979 and the old members' structure extensively refurbished in 1990-91. The memorial gates honour the early amateur C.J.T. Poole.

While Northants have won three one-day trophies and several times threatened seriously in the championship, the most remarkable feats have come from visiting players. Kent's Blythe took 17 wickets for 48 in 1907 while Percy Fender of Surrey hammered the fastest first-class century off legitimate bowling, taking only 35 minutes in 1920.

Getting There

Rail: Northampton.
Buses: 1, 51.
Road: Ground is north-east of town centre. From A45 take A5095 (Rushmere Road) then left into Wellingborough Road (A4500). Wantage Road first on right. From centre take A4500 Wellingborough Road.

Old Trafford

Old Trafford, Warwick Road, Manchester M16 0PX
Tel: 0161 282 4000
Capacity: 20,500
Matches: West Indies v Australia, 30 May; Super Six match, 8 June; First semi-final, 16 June

Second only to Lord's in capacity, Old Trafford holds British cricket's all-time crowd record, with 46,000 squeezing on to its terraces for the 1926 Roses match. It is also the second longest-standing English Test venue, predating Lord's by a fortnight in 1884, and has since staged 63 Tests. The pavilion, square-on to the wicket and second only to Lord's as the most recognizable cricketing structure on these shores, was constructed in 1894, by which time the ground had been Lancashire's headquarters for 29 years.

Lancashire have yet to follow the practice of other counties in renaming stands after local heroes – accommodation is austerely lettered A to K. The ground is permanently lodged in cricket lore as the venue for Jim Laker's 19 wickets against Australia in 1956. While it has staged eight World Cup matches, none has made the impact of that 1971 Gillette Cup semi-final, reflecting Lancashire's own pre-eminence in one-day cricket. The NatWest final victory over Derbyshire in 1998 represented the club's 14th limited-overs title in 30 seasons.

Getting There

Rail: Old Trafford (Manchester Metrolink).
Buses: 52, 53, 115. Any bus down Chester Road.
Road: From M60 junction 7, take A56 towards Manchester. Fork right onto A5067 (Talbot Road) and ground on right. From city centre take A56 south, fork left onto A5067.

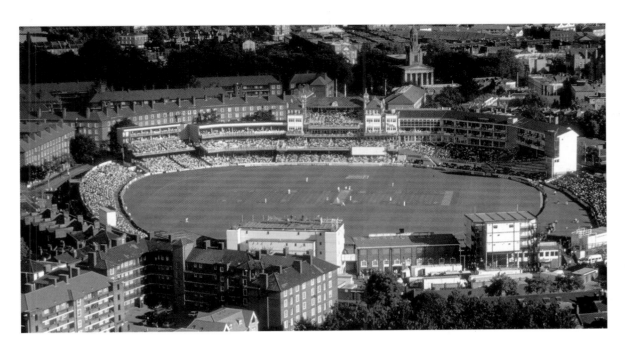

The Oval

The Oval, Kennington, London SE11 5SS
Tel: 0171 582 6660
Capacity: 19,000
Matches: England v South Africa, 22 May; Super Six match, 4 June; Super Six match, 11 June

Matier and more democratic, The Oval is South London's counterpart to Lord's. Like Wellington's Basin Reserve a giant traffic island and still, in spite of extensive and spectacular redevelopment at the Pavilion End, visually unmistakable because of the gasholders and Archbishop Tenison's Grammar School flanking the ground. The view from the pavilion has changed, with the giant MI6 building at Vauxhall now more noticeable than the Houses of Parliament. England's first home Test venue – in 1880 – was also the location for the first FA Cup final in 1872 and the 19 that followed between 1874 and 1892. More recently, on account of the largest (170m x 150m) playing surface in England, it has staged Australian Rules exhibition matches.

Its traditional (if not invariable) role as the stage for the final Test of the summer has given it some of the game's most memorable moments, the reclamation of the Ashes in 1926 and 1953 possibly the most fondly remembered. Regarded as a batsman's paradise it has nevertheless seen some memorable bowling in recent years, most notably Devon Malcolm's nine-wicket, 'You guys are history' destruction of the 1994 South Africans and, at the other end of the pace scale, Muttiah Muralitharan's extraordinary 16-wicket effort for Sri Lanka last year. Eight matches, including three semi-finals, were staged here in the first three World Cups. West Indies won all five they played here, including three semi-finals.

Getting There

Rail: Vauxhall.
London Underground: Oval, Vauxhall.
Buses: 3, 36, 109, 133, 155, 159, 185.
Road: Ground is half a mile south of Vauxhall Bridge on the A202 Vauxhall Road, close to the junction of the A3 and A23.

Southampton

The County Cricket Ground, Northlands Road, Southampton SO15 2UE
Tel: 01703 333788
Capacity: 4700
Matches: West Indies v New Zealand, 24 May; Sri Lanka v Kenya, 30 May

The ground that probably won't be there by the time of the next World Cup. Hampshire's development plans for new premises at West End, Southampton, aimed to be in operation by 2001, will rely in part for funding on the sale of Northlands Road. A £7.2m lottery grant has been awarded for a multi-sports facility which will include a 10,000-capacity cricket ground. The first phase, the laying down of the squares and nets, was underway by the end of 1997 under the supervision of Nigel Gray, Groundsman of the Year in 1995 and 1998, for his consistently good squares at Southampton.

Northlands Road has been Hampshire's headquarters since 1885 and the pavilion dates from 1896 – its bell is a relic of Southampton's maritime traditions, coming from the Cunard liner Athlone Castle. The ground staged a World Cup match in 1983 and looked likely to see a shock when Houghton and Curran put on 103 in 17 overs for Zimbabwe against Australia. But the later batting failed, leaving Australia relieved winners by 32 runs. Hampshire's one-day records are dominated by Gordon Greenidge, whose most spectacular onslaught was 177 in a total of 371 for four – both 60-over records at the time – against Glamorgan in 1975.

Getting There

Rail: Southampton Central.
Buses: 5, 14B, 16.
Road: From M3 take A33 into Southampton, following yellow AA signs. Ground is approximately 1.5 miles north of city centre, first turning on the right at the end of Southampton Common.

Taunton

The Clerical Medical County Ground, St James's Street, Taunton, Somerset TA1 1JT
Tel: 01823 272946
Capacity: 5700
Matches: Zimbabwe v Kenya, 15 May; Sri Lanka v India, 26 May

Visually spectacular at either end, offering the choice of four church towers or the Quantock Hills, which double as an informal weather forecast service – local opinion holding firmly that if you can't see them, rain is imminent. Described by Geoffrey Moorhouse in 1978 as a ground where 'the rustic image does come true... charmingly... haphazardly cobbled together over a century or more'. Moorhouse was writing immediately before Somerset's most successful era, when Richards and Botham made them briefly the most glamorous team in England, and 88 trophy-less years were followed by five one-day titles in as many seasons.

The ground is much improved since then, but the charm remains. The memorial gates commemorate slow-left-armer J.C. White whose patience and cunning over 28 years in the county colours are attested to by the slew of batting records associated with Taunton: English cricket's first two quadruple centuries, by Archie MacLaren in 1895 and Graeme Hick in 1988, Jack Hobbs surpassing W.G.'s career record of 126 centuries in 1925 plus the little matter of a Richards 322 in 1985. The previous World Cup match at Taunton in 1983 produced 619 runs, leaving Sri Lanka's captain Arjuna Ranatuga with mixed memories after scoring 34 and conceding 65 runs in England's 47-run victory.

Getting There

Rail: Taunton. Ground is very close to bus station.
Road: From M5 take junction 25, A358, then join A38 towards town centre. At roundabout take Priory Avenue (A3038), straight over next roundabout into Priory Bridge Road. Ground on left.

Most Catches in a Match (fielders only)

Clive Lloyd	3	West Indies v Sri Lanka, Manchester 1975
Dermot Reeve	3	England v Pakistan, Adelaide 1992
Ijaz Ahmed, sen.	3	Pakistan v Australia, Perth 1992
Allan Border	3	Australia v Zimbabwe, Hobart 1992
Chris Cairns	3	New Zealand v UAE, Faisalabad 1996

Most Dismissals in a Match

Syed Kirmani	5	India v Zimbabwe, Leicester 1983
Jimmy Adams	5	West Indies v Kenya, Pune 1996
Rashid Latif	5	Pakistan v New Zealand, Lahore 1996

Trent Bridge

Trent Bridge, Bridgford Road, Nottingham, NG2 6AG
Tel: 0115 982 1525
Capacity: 15,000
Matches: England v Zimbabwe, 25 May; Super Six match, 5 June; Super Six match 12 June

'It has managed to achieve the perfect balance between a stadium and a less ambitious cricket ground where players and watchers are blended into one. It is palatial compared with The Oval or Headingley, but it lacks the studied grandeur of Lord's, has more charm than Old Trafford and is instinct with history that has eluded Edgbaston so far.' Geoffrey Moorhouse stated the definitive case for Trent Bridge 20 years ago. The irony is that this is a ground founded by one remarkable bowler – William Clarke, founder of the early Victorian touring All England XI, who took over the Trent Bridge Inn in 1838 – and which has stands named after two others, Harold Larwood and Bill Voce, yet until pitch relaying restored the balance in the Fifties, was renowned as a batsman's dream. 'A lotus-land for action,' wrote Neville Cardus, 'a place where it was always afternoon and 360 for two.'

    Trent Bridge's concern for its current public is reflected in recent redevelopment and the most informative scoreboard in the game, as well as its concern for its past in the magnificent library maintained by Peter Wynne-Thomas in the evocative Victorian pavilion. The ground celebrates the centenary of its first Test – W.G.'s last – in June 1999. Zimbabwe will be happy to return to the site of their first World Cup victory.

Getting There

Rail: Nottingham.
Buses: 1, 2a, 10, 12, 29a, 71, 90.
Road: Near junction of A52 and A60, across Trent Bridge from city centre. Leave M1 at junction 25. Well signposted.

Worcester

County Ground, New Road, Worcester WR2 4QQ
Tel: 01905 748474
Capacity: 4400
Matches: Australia v Scotland, 16 May; Zimbabwe v Sri Lanka, 22 May

By general consent the most beautiful ground in England, with its fourteenth-century cathedral providing perhaps the best-known image of the county game, New Road celebrates its centenary this year. The ground authorities will hope to be better prepared than in 1899 when the sightscreens were still being painted on the morning of the first match.

The ground is well accustomed to invaders, whether in the shape of the River Severn, which has regularly inundated it during winters – in 1947 flooding the pavilion, which like most New Road buildings is raised on stilts, to a depth of three and a half feet – or the touring teams for whom it was the first stop for much of this century. Worcester hosted Bradman's first innings in England – a double century in 1930, followed by two repeat performances and a valedictory 100 in 1948. It has mixed memories for the teams in its second match this year: Sri Lanka offered the first definitive proof of their superiority to other non-Test nations in 1979 by beating Canada here to take the inaugural ICC Trophy, but four years later Zimbabwe were comprehensively defeated by West Indies, spearheaded by a century from Greenidge.

Getting There

Rail: Worcester Foregate St.
Buses: 23, 44, 46.
Road: Follow AA signs for Worcester Races towards City Centre. Take Bridge Street (A38) and go left over Bridge, continue down New Road (A44), ground on left.

Most Catches (fielders only)

Name	Catches
Clive Lloyd (West Indies)	12
Desmond Haynes (West Indies)	12
Kapil Dev (India)	12
Chris Cairns (New Zealand)	10
Ian Botham (England)	10
Allan Border (Australia)	10
Javed Miandad (Pakistan)	10
Sanath Jayasuriya (Sri Lanka)	9
Allan Lamb (England)	9
Viv Richards (West Indies)	9
Kris Srikkanth (India)	9

World Cup Records 1975-96

Chapter 7

A Side of Beef

World Cup Select XII 1975-96

Author's Note: The players in this World Cup Select XII have been nominated by an all-seeing selection committee of one. The committee would like to point out that the following XII would give them a stern fight: Turner (G), Greenidge, Crowe (M), Zaheer, Gower, Border (capt), Dujon (wkt), Kapil Dev, Holding, Mushtaq Ahmed, McDermott and Rhodes (J). The committee would also like to point out that of the dozen names below, at least half would also adorn a Test XII covering the same period. Which merely goes to show that the disciplines aren't as far apart as some like to pretend.

Sanath Jayasuriya (Sri Lanka)

Had Jackson Pollock taken up cricket he would have played it this way. Anybody with the sheer unmitigated gall to launch his first ball in a Test for six, and win the match in the process, is clearly a rather special fellow. The last World Cup confirmed just how special.

There had been scant warning. Short of stature and backlift, this chunky, amply-shouldered left-hander from the fishing town of Matara had flitted in and out of the national team since his Test debut in 1990-91. And up and down the order. Unsure whether to be true to instinct or adapt and compromise, he brought to mind the ancient quip about that erstwhile New Zealand new-ball

operative, Bob Cunis – neither one thing nor the other. Opening in the 1995-6 Benson & Hedges World Series against Australia and West Indies, indeed, he had cobbled together 173 runs at 17.30, highest score 30.

Neither did an inconspicious overture to the tournament prepare us. In Delhi against India, though, everything suddenly clicked as he and the similarly free-spirited Kaluwitherana shot past 40 inside the opening three overs; by the time he was out for 79 he had had the good grace to slow down. Against Kenya, the openers flashed and dashed to 83 in eight overs. When 'Kalu' departed early in the quarter-final against England, his partner in criminal irreverence set off on an improvisational solo that would have turned Charlie Parker green, thrashing 82 off 44 balls, each cut and drive a raspberry blown. Despite failing to broach double figures in the semi-final or final he was still a runaway nominee as the tournament's Most Valuable Player. 'He challenged our assumptions,' wrote David Hopps in *Wisden*. The approach to playing himself in appeared to comprise a skip, a jump and a carve over cover.

In Singapore a few weeks later, he celebrated with a flourish (as if that were possible), lighting up the Singer Cup with the most explosive and sustained bout of hitting the form had yet witnessed. Uncowed when Pakistan asked Sri Lanka to bat, he hustled to 50 in 32 balls then roared to three figures in half that many, surpassing Kapil Dev's record pace by no fewer than 14 deliveries. In the final, facing the same testing foes, he whizzed to 50 off his 17th ball, erasing Simon O'Donnell's world mark; when Kaluwitherana was dismissed in the sixth over, for a duck, he had swept to 66; by the time Pakistan had got shot of him he had whizzed to 76 off 28 balls. No teammate reached 35.

Firmly established at last, the following year saw him unveil another facet of his personality, helping Sri Lanka attain the distinction of being the first representative side to come within 50 runs of a four-figure total; his was the lion's share, a relatively restrained 340 spanning two days. Throw in that nigglesome left-arm spin – in the World Cup semi-final he outfoxed Tendulkar and two other specialists at a cost of a dozen runs – plus a seemingly permanent grin, *et voilà:* a man for all reasons.

Mark Waugh (Australia)

Cooler than a frozen cucumber, insufferably insouciant. He records every century on his lucky thigh pad much as a fighter pilot notches kills on the side of his cockpit, and usually bats like he bets, with a millionaire's devil-may-carelessness. Rechristened 'Afghanistan' – the Forgotten Waugh – amid those initial struggles in the shadow of his more sombre twin, this languid, leg-side-favouring New South Walian leaves indelible impressions every time he moseys to the middle: seductive of stroke, serene of temperament, no present-day cricketer makes run-making look so nauseatingly simple.

Everything you need to know about Waugh Minor was there to be relished on his Test debut, coming as it did fully five years after Steve's. Unconcerned at coming in at 104 for four, he straight-drove his second ball for four; in the space of 11 deliveries from Phil Tufnell's orthodox left-arm slows he reeled off five further boundaries. He was progressing at very nearly a run a ball when he arrived at three figures. It seems he had taken the advice of his pal Robin Smith to heart. As he prepared to face his first ball, Smith, fielding for England, whispered, 'Now's the time to release the handbrake, champ.' It has seldom been on since.

An increasingly useful all-rounder, besides being the lithest of predators close to the wicket – no peer in the slips can touch him – he serves up a mean bumper, while his off-spin has matured with growing conviction. Sufficiently, certainly, to dispatch Lara, Richardson and Arthurton at Jaipur during the last World Cup. Wielding brush rather than broadsword, he also spent those weeks proving timing to be as efficacious as strength when it comes to taking appropriate toll of fielding restrictions.

More aggressive, not say productive, after moving up to open from his habitual Test slot of four, Australia's first three outings saw him string together a sequence of 130, 126 and 76 not out, then douse New Zealand's hopes in the last eight with another sublime century. Sri Lanka were indeed fortunate that Vaas made short work of him in the final: the havoc such a destroyer of spin might have wreaked on that moderate twirler-studded attack didn't bear contemplating. The betting scandal tarnished his name but the glow endures. If Rembrandt had taken up cricket he would have played it this way.

Viv Richards (West Indies)

Short of Freddie Krueger donning helmet and pads, it is difficult to envisage a cricketer doing more to immobilize the opposition through sheer fright. Has any batsman ever beaten so many bowlers while adjusting his box? More Marvin Hagler than Marvan Atapattu, intimidating from the instant he embarked on that stately, bicep-swinging, shoulder-flexing, oh-so superior saunter to the crease, Isaac Vivian Alexander Richards deserved every syllable of his regal name.

Passionate, independent and assuredly no forelock-tugger, yet fiercely proud of his African roots, he saw cricket as a means of advancing island unity – and hence succeeding where the politicians had failed – as well as black awareness. He was inspired, warranted Frank Tyson, the England quick bowler-turned-writer, 'by a mixture of pride and prejudice'. Many was the time he would glance up in despair at the disparate flags fluttering above the stands in Bridgetown, Kingston and his native Antigua, embarrassed and infuriated by the sight of such graphic disunity.

Three instances of that audacious power stand out. There he was, grabbing the 1979 final by the scruff of the neck and shaking all the competition from it. There was that 56-ball blast against England before his Antiguan kith and kin

in 1986, the speediest of all Test centuries. Between times came the most dominant one-day knock of all. At Old Trafford in 1984, toying with a more than presentable England attack that had reduced his side to 102 for seven and 166 for nine, he muscled his way to 93 out of an unbroken last-wicket stand of 106 compiled at more than seven runs an over, and wound up with 189 off 170 balls. More than a decade would elapse before Saeed Anwar became the first man in limited-overs internationals to reach the 190s.

Not that he confined himself to one cause. More even than Botham, here was the match that lit Somerset's fire. In the 1979 Gillette Cup final he was almost exclusively responsible for the total that ultimately earned the county their first trophy, whistling up 117 (no colleague reached 42); the 1981 Benson & Hedges Cup final brought an unconquered 132 (no colleague reached 40). In 1993, though in his forties and with eyesight fading, he inspired Glamorgan to the Sunday League title, his presence alone worth a 30-run start. Verily, the King of Antigua.

Sachin Tendulkar (India)

That rarest of beasts: the self-fulfilling prodigy. First capped at 16, before he was eighteen he had already saved two Tests, come within an ace of being crowned as the tenderest-footed centurian in five-day annals and had his sunnily handsome features displayed on bedroom walls from Madras to Maharashtra. Nor did it go to his head. He has become the most fêted man in India, captain (briefly) of his country and the first player to reap 20 hundreds in one-day internationals. Nobody involved in the impending festivities provokes quite the same sense of goose-bumping anticipation. Nobody, come to think of it, occupies the same planet. As Martin Crowe, no mean performer himself, put it, 'He plays like God'.

More correct and focused than Lara, his only contemporary rival as the world's most inventive, least stoppable batsman, he displayed his genius most powerfully against Australia last year. Knowing all too well that somebody had to do something about that pesky chap Warne before he exerted his customary stranglehold, he launched a premeditated onslaught that shredded the Victorian's confidence, punctured the tourists' morale and consigned them to their first defeat in 10 Test rubbers.

Surprisingly, he had a relatively sluggish start in the limited-overs fray (at one time that clever brew of spin and seam-up loomed as a more potent asset) but all that came to an abrupt end in 1994, when, having insisted upon opening the innings against New Zealand, he sped to 82 off 49 balls. Come the World Cup two years later he was simply irresistible. In the group stage he made 127 not out against Kenya, 70 against West Indies, 90 against Australia and 137 against Sri Lanka, amassing 427 runs at an average of 106.75; in only one of those innings was a bowler responsible for his ejection. A mortal 31 in the quarter-final against Pakistan was followed by a top-scoring if fruitless 65 in the semi against the buoyant Sri Lanka. His final tally of 523 runs constituted a new tournament record.

Nor has he dithered since. Last year, freer of spirit after giving up the captaincy, he collected a century and the Man of the Match award to decide the destiny of both the Independence Cup in Calcutta and the Coca-Cola Cup in Colombo. The most sobering thought for the world's bowlers is that he enters World Cup 99 at the ripe old age of 26.

Highest Totals

398 for 5	**Sri Lanka v Kenya**, Kandy 1996
360 for 4	**West Indies v Sri Lanka**, Karachi 1987
338 for 5	**Pakistan v Sri Lanka**, Swansea 1983
334 for 4	**England v India**, Lord's 1975
333 for 9	**England v Sri Lanka**, Taunton 1983
330 for 6	**Pakistan v Sri Lanka**, Nottingham 1975
328 for 3	**South Africa v Holland**, Rawalpindi 1996
328 for 5	**Australia v Sri Lanka**, The Oval 1975
322 for 6	**England v New Zealand**, The Oval 1983
321 for 2	**South Africa v UAE**, Rawalpindi 1996

Javed Miandad (Pakistan)

'I was surprised he left one stump standing.' Thus did Kim Hughes, Australia's captain, make light of Rodney Hogg's demolition of his own wicket upon his dismissal against Pakistan in 1979. Hogg had been innocently prodding the pitch, or so it was alleged, when Javed sneaked in to run him out, the arch-competitor at his archest.

Whether threatening provocateurs with an upraised bat, or struggling for acceptance as captain of his country knowing that Imran Khan, a chap a good couple of rungs higher up the class ladder, would swan back to relieve him whenever he deigned to make himself available, Pakistan's (and the World Cup's) most prolific batsman always seemed to have his fists cocked. And not exclusively in the figurative sense. A flea in the ear of every opponent, he was the grinning, streetwise streetfighter who never gave a millimetre or acknowledged a lost cause.

Enlisted by his country at 17, having already made 311 for Karachi Whites, this chirpy welterweight impressed more with leg-breaks than leg-glides during the inaugural World Cup. Eight months of his teens still remained when he became Test cricket's callowest double-centurian. Hired by Sussex, he was initially regarded in some quarters as impetuous, but compensations soon became abundantly clear.

One of the youngest of the Packer 'rebels', he left Sussex for Glamorgan in 1980 following a season-long slump and proceeded to astonish his new colleagues as soon as he docked at Cardiff. 'Without any kit or clothes of his own, [he] took guard in a practice game and despatched all and sundry to various parts of the ground,' marvelled leg-spinner Robin Hobbs. 'His first innings was against Essex at Swansea, where, on a rain-affected pitch, he tore the formidable Essex attack to ribbons, scoring 140 not out. The daring of his strokeplay and the brilliance of his improvisation were a revelation.' The next most robust

Aravinda de Silva

contribution that day was 24. Footloose, nerve-free and a withering cutter, reverse sweeps and pulls were his stock-in-trade long before they became hip.

Creative and restless, a bottomless box of tricks in the limited-overs lash, yet patient where appropriate, he made his presence felt in six World Cups, the only man so to do, durability personified. The 1992 tourney, wherein he briefly led the side in Imran's absence, was a personal *tour de force* despite his being dogged by injury, 437 runs at an average of 62 culminating in that decisive stand with his nemesis in the final. Far better an ally than an enemy.

All-Rounders *Qualification: 50 Runs and 3 Wickets in a Match*

Name		Runs	Wickets
Majid Khan	Pakistan v Australia, Nottingham 1979	61	3-53
Duncan Fletcher	Zimbabwe v Australia, Nottingham 1983	★ 69	4-42
Kevin Curran	Zimbabwe v India, Tunbridge Wells 1983	73	3-65
Mohammad Azharuddin	India v Australia, Delhi 1987	★ 54	3-19
Imran Khan	Pakistan v Australia, Lahore 1987	58	3-36
Ian Botham	England v Australia, Sydney 1992	53	4-31
Peter Kirsten	South Africa v Zimbabwe, Canberra 1992	★ 62	3-31
Aravinda de Silva	Sri Lanka v Australia, Lahore 1996	★ 107	3-42

World Cup Records 1975-96

Aravinda de Silva (Sri Lanka)

The only man to be anointed Man of the Match in the semi-finals and final of the same World Cup, this slightly-built son of Colombo picked up the baton from Jayasuriya and transported Sri Lanka to the summit. More feline than leonine, those sublimely supple strokes mask an outwardly mild soul driven by patriotism, indignation and a fondness for fast cars.

Developing bravura through the auspices of a weekend club league whose demands echoed those in England's Sunday League, he resolved not to let anything pass outside off-stump unmolested. That said, though a far from incompetent off-spinner to boot, he took time to adjust to loftier stages. Then again, keeping mind and body focused for a couple of games a year, as was so often the case in the 1980s, was, as Australians so succinctly put it, a big ask.

His first season in the English shires in 1995 broadened the fan base considerably. Unfazed at being part of a Kent unit propping up the championship table, he totted up 1,781 enriching runs at an average of nearly 60, underlining his nervelessness by taking the Man of the Match award for a 95-ball 112 in the Benson & Hedges Cup final: as the author of the grandest innings by a Lord's loser, he deserved nothing less. 'The ball was feathered not bludgeoned, persuaded not carved,' celebrated Ivo Tennant in *Wisden*. 'I cannot believe any player, anywhere, has been so popular,' marvelled Graham Cowdrey, a Canterbury confrère whose own confidence he revived. 'Ari was an inspiration to me and the whole side felt the same. When he packed his bags, he hugged each of us and I have never known a professional sports team so close to tears.'

The next year brought fulfilment. In the Calcutta semi-final, wrote Mike Marqusee, 'the ball was his to do with as he willed'. In 1998 he was back at Lord's for the Princess Diana Memorial match, outdazzling the game's most glittering assets, even Tendulkar. He is 33 and at the zenith of his powers. For de Silva, the best, unthinkably, may be yet to come.

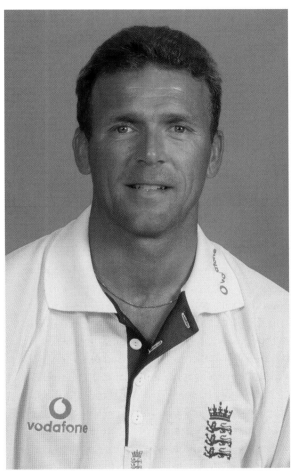

Alec Stewart (England, wicket-keeper)

A contentious and parochial choice (it would be the height of bad manners, surely, not to include a single representative of the host nation), admittedly his selection is based as much on what the England captain may yet achieve as on the derring-dos he has already perpetrated.

An agelessly agile performer who would hardly look out of place propelling himself between the sticks at his beloved Stamford Bridge, Stewart is 36 going on 27. How improbable it now seems that this supremely fit, fastidious orange juice fiend could once have been accused of having earned selection through nepotism. Forget, for a moment, that strutting bat, 'The Gaffer' submits rip-roaring proof of a theory propounded by a fellow picker-up of gauntlets, the Australian colossus Rod Marsh, that the best stumpers improve with age.

The term wicket-keeper/batsman is commonly employed to refer to those, notably Alan Knott, Healy and Marsh himself, who supplement their gilded glovework with feistiness at the crease. Dujon, a princely stroke-player who first appeared for West Indies as a specialist batsman, became an eminently capable keeper; Stewart has done likewise – only more so. The first bona fide batsman/wicket-keeper? Not quite, since Les Ames and Jim Parks also deserved such a sobriquet, but a special talent just the same.

Granted, his technique standing up to the spinners has never been quite as coolly assured as that of Jack Russell, the subject of a Campaign for Real Wicket-keepers that reached a crescendo when Stewart got the nod ahead of the noted teabag aficionado for the 1992-93 tour of India and Sri Lanka. But fortunately for Stewart, what few spinners have prospered for England in previous World Cups have rarely coaxed the ball to turn away from the right-hander – his *bête noire*. In all other respects he is a model of the craft, as spring-heeled as any standing back.

His potency, though, remains with the willow. In five successive games in 1992, arguably England's most memorable World Cup campaign to date, he was responsible for the side's highest or second-highest score. Taking the Man of the Match award with an aggressive but judicious 77 against South Africa, he played as if the load he was carrying – keeper, opener and skipper – were but gnats on that straight, unbending back, that trusty blade a tail with which to flick them away. If a blip in form made him markedly less prolific four years later, the return of Russell, combined with a wasteful slot in the middle-order, cannot have been unconnected. Here, after all, is a man who thrives on burdens; he feels naked without them.

His strength of purpose is said to have stemmed from his mother: when Alec first played for his school team, recounted father Micky, she would steel him against failure by threatening to deny him dinner. The impending hostilities constitute his tallest order to date; to discount his chances of carrying it out would be to ignore all the evidence.

Imran Khan (Pakistan, captain)

Most chaps thought him haughty. Others, such as Botham and Lamb, were less flattering, taking him to court over some disparaging comments about their lack of 'class'. The chapesses flocked to him like iron filings to a magnet. Yet those conversant with his principal claim to fame are as one: the game has produced few more commanding all-rounders, fast bowlers or even captains. By common consent, moreover, he was the only man who could have welded Pakistan's panoply of mercurial and factious talents into a cohesive, winning whole.

The ability to distance himself was crucial. Educated in his native Lahore and later at Worcester and Oxford, that well of self-belief evidently bottomless, this was by no means especially tricky. A magisterial influence at Sussex and Worcestershire, he led his country in 48 Tests in addition to the lion's share of his 175 one-day internationals, overseeing an era that saw Pakistan emerge as the one side equipped to take on West Indies without trepidation. So intrinsic was he considered, he was able to refuse to appear in domestic fixtures because he objected to the way the game was run in his homeland.

He also achieved the balance that eludes so many purported 'all-rounders': he was worth his place in both disciplines, averaging more than half as much again with the bat in Tests as he did with the ball (37 to 22). Not even Botham managed that. In one-dayers, only Steve Waugh and Kapil Dev have matched him in exceeding 175 wickets and 3,500 runs (and from far fewer games). But nobody can match his bag of 34 World Cup wickets.

He snared 17 victims at 13 runs a shot in 1987 but saved the *pièce de résistance* for the next tournament, by which time he was in his 40th year and apparently more concerned with constructing a hospital than a winning team. Having more or less hand-picked the side, injury confined him to walk-on roles in the early matches; returning against India, and reclaiming the captain's armband, he was run out for a duck. Then came a partial throwback to his bowling pomp, control now superseding speed; a restraining influence in the loss to South Africa, and then again in the defeat of Australia that began to transform his team's step from wary tread to expectant strut. Entering at first-drop in the semi-final against New Zealand he paved the way for Inzamam's conclusive assault with rare diligence. The final chapter is now enshrined in the hearts of millions, ensuring him the topmost plinth in his young nation's sporting pantheon, above even that squillionaire of the squash court, Jahangir Khan. The last of the dictator captains? Maybe. Either way, it is quite likely that we shall never glimpse his like again.

Joel Garner (West Indies)

No Marshall, Holding or Roberts, nor even an Ambrose or Walsh, all of whose undoubted qualities were more admirably suited to an arena wherein bouncers are legitimate, slips can be packed and bowlers do the intimidating. Only one member of the fabled Caribbean pace squadron makes the cut here, and much the most unusual of the lot at that.

Standing six foot eight in his capacious socks,

Joel Garner

'Big Bird' occupied a branch of his own when it came to cutting an innings off at the knees. Most gainfully employed in the latter stages, his yorker was the most irresistible of weapons, defying defence, let alone a counter-attack. And never more tellingly than when this wry, gentle, soon-to-be social worker bullied West Indies to their second World Cup.

Competent enough with lumps of wood to have claimed co-authorship of the tournament-record last-wicket stand of 71, as well as a prehensile presence in the gully, 'Big Bird' used every one of those 80 inches (plus another couple of dozen if one takes into account the stratospheric release point) to bamboozle batsmen. Two hundred and fifty-nine scalps in Tests at 20.59 apiece, one of the most consistently penetrative records of all time, stand testimony to the constancy of his power. It was in the abridged game, nevertheless, that he made his most vivid incisions.

Lord's had a habit of bringing out that fee-fi-fo-fum. In June 1979 he extinguished any lingering home hopes by taking five of the last six

Abdul Qadir

Highest Team Scores (batting second)

313 for 7	**Sri Lanka v Zimbabwe**, New Plymouth 1992	
289 for 4	**Australia v New Zealand**, Madras 1996	
288 for 9	**Sri Lanka v Pakistan**, Swansea 1983	
286	**Sri Lanka v England**, Taunton 1983	
276 for 3	**West Indies v Australia**, Lord's 1983	
276 for 4	**Sri Lanka v Australia**, The Oval 1975	
274	**Australia v West Indies**, Lord's 1975	
272 for 4	**Sri Lanka v India**, Delhi 1996	
269	**India v Australia**, Madras 1987	
267 for 9	**West Indies v Pakistan**, Birmingham 1975	

England's best second innings score
246 for 8 v West Indies, Gujranwala 1987

wickets for four runs in 11 balls, his yorker so lethal he clean bowled four of the Englishmen whose blood and wariness he'd scented. On that same grand stage three months later, this time sporting the Somerset gryphon, he did likewise to Northamptonshire, taking 6 for 29, including three bowled and one hit wicket. 'The only consolation of being bowled by Garner,' attested Scyld Berry, 'is that you haven't been hit on the boot.'

Abdul Qadir (Pakistan)

The man behind the man. Before Shane there was Abdul, the imp from the east with the black locks of a Stuart monarch and much the same capacity to offend the puritan.

Fiery and demonstrative, he once waded into the crowd in Barbados to sort out a heckler. Another time he was sent home from New Zealand for what were officially described as 'disciplinary' reasons. Nor did his appealing appeal to the fuddy and the duddy. Voluble, occasionally histrionic and never less than theatrical, he did not so much implore umpires as dare them to reject him. Body contorted, arms flailing in a manner

eerily reminiscent of Kermit the frog, he looked for all the world like a puppet who had just snipped his strings. Beneath the showman, though, lurked a roomy sleeve and oodles of rabbits: a rubbery wrist, a tirelessly inventive mind, a substantial repertoire, a boyish zest and a fast bowler's snarl.

Prior to his breakthrough to wider consciousness on Pakistan's 1982 tour to England, it bears remembering, wrist-spin had spent the best part of three decades not so much out of fashion as out of circulation. A rash of turgid, seamer-friendly pitches was mostly to blame but the general dearth of adventure from the Fifties to early Seventies wasn't far behind. True, Richie Benaud, Intikhab Alam, Mushtaq Mohammad and the freakishly unorthodox Bhagwat Chandrasekar had their days, but in a conservative, pace-obsessed game, off-spin, safe and solid, became the option of preference. Abdul Qadir Khan retrieved the ball and ran with it.

Besides the conventional leg-break, his arsenal contained a googly, a flipper and two different top-spinners, all delivered with that whirring, flamboyant action. None more distinctive, surely, has been witnessed in the name of artful dodgery. As the prancing approach gave way to a series of dainty skips and hops, elbows would wag, the mane tossed with disdain. You

Best Career Economy Rates
Qualification: 300 balls bowled

Name	Balls	R	W	Avge	Best	5w	Econ
Bishen Bedi (India)	360	148	2	74.00	1-6	–	2.46
Mike Hendrick (England)	336	149	10	14.90	4-15	–	2.66
Bob Willis (England)	709	315	18	17.50	4-11	–	2.66
Chris Old (England)	543	243	16	15.18	4-8	–	2.68
Richard Hadlee (New Zealand)	877	421	22	19.13	5-25	1	2.88
Michael Holding (West Indies)	695	341	20	17.05	4-33	–	2.94
Bernard Julien (West Indies)	360	177	10	17.70	4-20	–	2.95
Venkat (India)	432	217	0	–	–	–	3.01
Malcolm Marshall (West Indies)	678	349	14	24.92	3-28	–	3.08
Vic Marks (England)	468	246	13	18.92	5-39	1	3.15

could have popped a feather on his head and backed him for gold in the Olympic dressage.

No mean smiter – as Courtney Walsh will painfully testify – his value to Pakistan's cause was eminently visible during the 1987 World Cup. Aided by the familiarity of the terrain – the previous tournament in England had been one of moderate personal fruits – he gleaned 12 scalps at 20 apiece while yielding barely three-and-a-half runs per over: the perfect package. Against England at Rawalpindi he came on as second-change, picked up three of the first five wickets and wound up with four for 31 together with the Man of the Match award. When the teams reconvened in Karachi he all but repeated the dose. Pity cockiness had to set in.

And there he was a few years later, on the hall rug at home in Lahore, availing his trade secrets to a like-minded Australian beach bum with earring and attitude. Warne still treasures such generosity. Arthur Mailey, the first of the immortal leggies from Down Under, was once scolded by his team manager for giving advice to Ian Peebles, a youthful Pommy practitioner. 'Slow bowling is an art, Mr Kelly,' Mailey retorted, 'and art is international.' Still bamboozling at 44 – and apparently with only marginally-reduced effervescence if his opponents in Melbourne grade cricket are to be believed – Abdul Qadir is cut from the same broad-minded cloth.

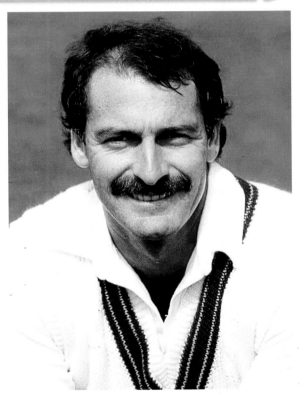

Dennis Lillee (Australia)

To the unbridled relief of thigh pads and forearm guards from Antigua to Yorkshire, the World Cup rarely wrung the best from him, denuding him as it did of slips, rendering that innate aggression more of a liability. At The Oval in 1975 he was at the sharp end of Kallicharran's cutlass, shipping runs at almost seven an over, lured into indiscretion by machismo, stubbornly refusing to resort to the

Most Dismissals (wicket-keepers)			
Name	**Dismissals**	**Ct**	**St**
Wasim Bari (Pakistan)	22	18	4
Ian Healy (Australia)	21	18	3
Jeff Dujon (West Indies)	20	19	1
Rod Marsh (Australia)	18	17	1
Kiran More (India)	18	12	6
Deryck Murray (West Indies)	16	16	0
Dave Richardson (South Africa)	15	14	1
Syed Kirmani (India)	14	12	2
David Williams (West Indies)	14	11	3
Moin Khan (Pakistan)	14	11	3

World Cup Records 1975-96

Roger Harper

pragmatic: the biter savaged. In 1979 he cobbled together four wickets at more than 40 apiece while surrendering four runs an over. Only at Headingley four years earlier did he truly stamp his authority, whisking out five Pakistanis for 34 – the tournament's inaugural five-fer – while greasing a slide from 181 for four to 205 all out. A peak amid a slew of troughs.

All the same, ask any batsman unfortunate enough to encounter him between 1970 and 1983 whom they would least like to see approaching from the other end and the answer would be unanimous. In 70 Tests he harvested 355 scalps, the most striking rate by any fast bowler this century. Nor, ultimately, was he demonstrably less overpowering in his 63 international one-dayers, reaping 102 victims at 20.82. From that dastardly moustache to the feet that once lashed out at Javed, here was a brazen anti-authoritarian oozing as much malevolence as self-belief. Yet the opposition were far more frequently out-thought than out-fought.

Overcoming a crippling back condition that would have compelled most others to seek a new vocation, he set a benchmark for resolution. Adjusting his action accordingly, slackening in pace while upping skill and stealth, Lillee Mark II evolved into one of the shrewdest bowlers ever to tread a sward, as apt to dumbfound with leg-break as off-cutter.

'The best fast bowler I have ever seen,' proclaimed Bob Willis, a fellow member of Test cricket's 300-wicket fraternity. 'He had everything: courage, variety, high morale, arrogance, supreme fitness and aggression.' Max Walker, who helped his compatriot pick off the Pakistanis in 1975, hailed him as 'the complete example of self-motivation'. Any bowler capable of wringing chants of 'Kill, kill, kill' is surely worth having on your side.

Roger Harper
(West Indies, 12th man)

To some this will bear more than a passing resemblance to heresy. How could anyone possibly overlook Jonty Rhodes, the human hoover? By recalling the heyday of 'The Harpoon', that's how.

Though long since reduced to the role of international irregular, this gangling Guyanan returned to the fore at the last World Cup, supplementing the penetration and control of those spidery off-breaks with more than a few telling tonks. He also reminded the world of his chief gift: an uncanny capacity to intercept any ball, any time, anywhere, anyhow.

In terms of cutting off runs, the focal point of every fielder in the pyjama game, hand-eye co-ordination is obviously a must, likewise speed, anticipation and a genuine hunger for the ball (though a penchant for playing cat to the batsmen's mice can be decidedly useful). The secret, revealed 'The Harpoon', lies not in bending the waist but the knees, 'and getting your bottom down low'. Having the talent to catch flies while blindfolded has also come in fairly handy.

Here, all the same, is a graph that has been more inclined to wane than wax. Though he is a genuine all-rounder with a first-class double century on his CV, a critic swayed by one-dimensional statistics might even deem Harper a failure. After leading Young West Indies to a 2-0 win in the 1982 'Test' series against their English hosts, graduation to the senior post seemed inevitable. Instead, he was plagued by the 'yips', losing potency with the ball. But few remember that. Whether in the cordon, covers or outfield, he elevated fielding to unsuspected realms of splendour.

However unintentionally – colleagues have certainly never regarded him as the selfish, self-seeking type – he has reserved his sauciest sorcery for his own bowling. During one-dayers for Northamptonshire, with six men swamping the leg-side, his off-side field would comprise a deep extra cover, a long-off and a point stationed inside the fielding circle. Which meant that, once he had delivered the ball, he was henceforth saddled with protecting the entire expanse in front of the wicket on the off-side. So telescopic was his reach, so swift his movements and sure his grasp, it was a risk taken without compunction.

It was at Lord's in 1987 that he conjured the most lasting image of the MCC Bicentenary Test, a gala occasion enhanced by all manner of bodacious batsmanship, but crowned by Harper's contribution to the time capsule. Observing that Graham Gooch advanced early when sashaying down the pitch to drive, he resolved to do another 'Inspector Glasgow', a reference to a jabbering batsman he once silenced while playing for Demerara against Police as a 16-year-old. Collecting Gooch's next venomous straight biff as if he were a goalkeeper halting a toepoke from the boot of a two-year-old, he hurled the ball back in the same flowing motion, an arrow heading unerringly for the bull. As leather toppled timber Gooch was spitting dust, out by a street, gob not so much smacked as well and truly middled. The scorecard read 'Gooch run out'; by rights, the entry should have been 'stumped & bowled Harper'.

Baseball has its designated hitter, a batter who never has to dirty his precious hands in the field. When cricket gets around to universally adopting the precise opposite (substitutes are already being used in South Africa and Australia, so we can safely rule out if), the debate over the prince of designated fielders will be over before it starts. Roger Harper, superman out of time.

World Cup Totals		World Cup Records 1975-96
Runs Scored	66,230	
Wickets Taken	2191	
Centuries	51	
Ducks	197	

Acknowledgements

Thank-you muchlys to: Steven Lynch (buck-passer supreme), Huw Richards (ground authority to the stars) for writing Chapter 6, *From Arundel to Zimbabwe* by Robin Osmond, Peter David Lush and Dave Farrar for directions used in Chapter 6, Gordon Vince for compiling the World Cup records, John Pawsey (agent to the Gods), those sweet photocopiers at the British Library, Jenny Olivier and all at Boxtree, plus anybody whose work I may have innocently (and respectfully) cribbed. And, of course, to the beings who have to suffer my obsession: Anne, Laura, Jojo and Evie, the latest addition to the attack.